PRINCE HARRY'S CURSE

First published 2025

Copyright in text © 2025 Robert Casey

Robert Casey asserts the right to be identified
as the author of this book.

This work is copyright but the text only may be used by others
provided that this work and Robert Casey are acknowledged as
the source of any quotation. Copyright in images remains with the
creator thereof.

ISBN 978-1-7641447-0-4

This book could not have been written without the excellent
skills of my friend Fred Baker. Thanks also to the many
people who provided images to platforms such as Wikipedia,
Facebook, YouTube and Twitter/X.
Sincere apologies if I have left out any names.

PRINCE HARRY'S CURSE

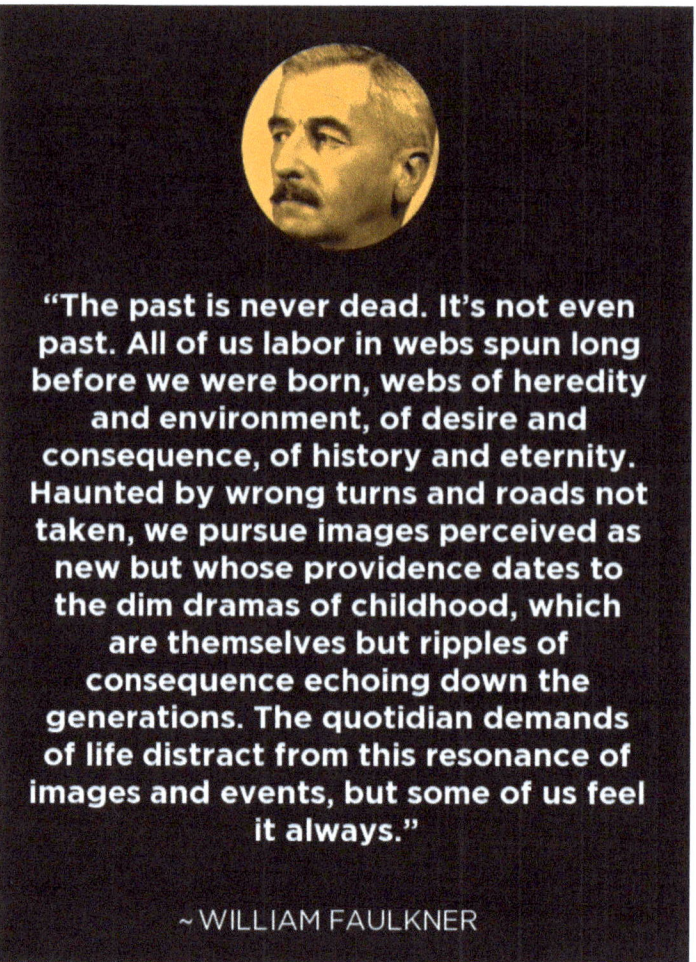

"The past is never dead. It's not even past. All of us labor in webs spun long before we were born, webs of heredity and environment, of desire and consequence, of history and eternity. Haunted by wrong turns and roads not taken, we pursue images perceived as new but whose providence dates to the dim dramas of childhood, which are themselves but ripples of consequence echoing down the generations. The quotidian demands of life distract from this resonance of images and events, but some of us feel it always."

~ WILLIAM FAULKNER

'THERE'S a very strange scene in *The Crown's* final episode about royal brothers from the 11th century. Prince William and Prince Harry discuss [hypothetical] plans for the Queen's abdication. 'That'd make you William the….' Harry says, before William chimes in 'Fifth.' 'Better than Second,' Harry replies. 'He was assassinated by his brother who, would you believe, was also called Prince Harry. He had William killed in a shooting "accident" and galloped off to Winchester to claim the thrown for himself. Don't worry, mate. I wouldn't do that to you.'

— Emily Burack, *Town and Country* (December 2023).

'HARRY, now a comfortable sixth in line to the throne, has forged his own path, looking for a life not dominated by his status as the second son. In breaking away from the royal family, he may finally have broken the curse of the spare, while his uncle Andrew's life lies in tatters.'

— Hadley Hall Meares, *Vanity Fair* (September 2021).

'PRINCE William views Prince Harry as a "curse on the monarchy", royal expert Tom Bower has revealed, claiming that in spite of the Duke's recent efforts to get back in contact with the royals there is little chance of their rift ending.'

Catherine Meyer-Funnell, *Daily Express* (November 2023)

'SCANDALOUS, doomed marriage of the ginger-haired Duke of Sussex and his older bride: No, NOT Harry and Meghan — but the only other regal couple to have shared their title.'

Daily Mail (May 2018)

CONTENTS

Foreword i

Introduction 1

1. The Curse of the Royal Spare 5
2. House of the Dragon 8
3. Sins of the Father 12
4. Descended from the Devil 16
5. 'They shall be childless' 20
6. Badges of Bastardy 24
7. The Masque of Blackness 28
8. The Curse of Ham 33
9. Harry's slave ancestor? 37
10. Theodore and Eliza 42
11. The Graveyard of Empires 47
12. Biblical Bloodlines 52
13. Harry, Hamlet and Freud 57
14. From Byron to Batman 63
15. 'The Past is Never Dead' 67
16. Something About Meghan? 72
17. Harry's Accursed Namesakes 76

Afterword 81

Foreword

LIKE Prince Harry's 2023 memoir *Spare,* this book starts with William Faulkner's well-known words about the past. But while Harry quoted only the first two sentences, it is well worth reading the entire passage from Faulkner's 1951 novel *Requiem for a Nun.* (The 'nun', by the way, was a black prostitute convicted of murdering a baby.)

When I started writing *Prince Harry's Curse,* I agonised about the title. Is he afflicted with one big, multi-layered curse or with multiple curses? In choosing the former, I have taken comfort from Faulkner's quote, and also from a lesser-known aphorism by Mark Twain: 'A favourite theory of mine is that no occurrence is sole and solitary, but is merely a repetition of a thing which has happened before, and perhaps often.'

It is truly amazing that nearly all of Harry's royal namesakes have been cursed, in one way or another, since Henry I allegedly murdered his older brother William Rufus in the New Forest in 1100, just one generation after King Harold (Prince William's nickname for Harry) was defeated by William the Bastard at the Battle of Hastings.

Prince Harry's accursedness is undeniable. In short, he is a red-headed royal spare, rumoured to be illegitimate, who is still suffering the trauma of his mother's death, plus agoraphobia and other mental disorders. As a member of the royal family, he is burdened with the racist legacies of slavery and imperialism, compounded because of Meghan's African ancestry and the 25 Taliban fighters Harry killed in Afghanistan.

Throw in alleged curses on Windsor and Spencer marriages, as well as the curse of celebrity in this age of social media, and Harry's life in exile is a never-ending nightmare. His brother hates him and he has been cut off from 'the sister he never had'. To make matters worse, both Princess Kate and his father have been diagnosed with cancer.

Regardless of Harry's afflictions, it can be argued that he is a curse on the monarchy — an opinion reportedly held by Prince William. Their great-grandmother had a similar opinion about Edward VIII: 'What a curse black sheep are in a family.' So, all things considered, the notion of a multi-layered curse on Harry is not far-fetched.

I am an Australian republican who sincerely hopes that Charles III is the last British monarch to be our head of state. That said, I have a certain fondness for Kate Middleton after spending several years writing *The Catherine Code* (2023). I am less fond of Prince Harry, for a variety of reasons, but I thank him profusely for providing so much to write about.

Bob Casey,
Hobart, Tasmania
July 2024

INTRODUCTION

Henry Charles Albert David Mountbatten-Windsor, commonly known as Prince Harry, is seemingly afflicted by a multilayered, interconnected curse with biblical overtones that began at the Battle of Hastings in 1066 when the English king Harold (which is Prince William's nickname for Harry) was defeated by William the Conqueror.

Three years later, Archbishop Aldred of York cursed the Conqueror (also known as William the Bastard) while he was 'harrying' England's north using scorched earth tactics that inspired similar violence in *Game of Thrones*. And because the first monarch was legally and morally bankrupt, the institution has arguably been cursed ever since.

Charles, Diana, William and Harry.

Nearly all of Prince Harry's royal namesakes were afflicted by curses, including the Angevin curse which pitted Henry the Young King against Henry II; the usurper's curse on Henry IV; the Windsor 'prophecy' which doomed Henry V and Henry VI; Philippa Gregory's 'King's Curse' which killed Henry VIII's first-born son Henry Cornwall; plus the famous Templar curse which afflicted the last five king Henrys.

Based on his ghostwritten 2023 memoir, simply titled *Spare*, the first layer of Prince Harry's curse was evident on the day he was born when Prince Charles told Princess Diana that, having delivered an heir and a spare, his 'work' was done. Charles then left the hospital to be with his mistress, now Queen Camilla.

'I was brought into the world in case something happened to Willy,' Harry wrote. 'I was summoned to provide backup, distraction, diversion and, if necessary, a spare part. Kidney, perhaps. Blood transfusion. Speck of bone marrow.' As one TikTok user pointed out, that was the plot of *My Sister's Keeper,* a 2004 novel by Jodi Picoult. And pity poor Diana because all she wanted was for Harry to be William's 'wingman'.

The second layer of Harry's curse emerged when Charles joked about his second son's rumoured illegitimacy. This matter could, and should, have been resolved years ago by DNA testing. Instead, millions of people now firmly believe that Harry was not sired by Charles III, which is especially noteworthy because Charles II had at least a dozen bastards but no legitimate children. Charles III does not descend from Charles II but Princess Diana had a bloodline from the Merry Monarch's bastard son Henry Fitzroy.

William Rufus

Henry I

LIKE his disgraced uncle and royal spare Prince Andrew, the current Duke of York — probably not sired by Elizabeth II's racing manager Lord Porchester — Harry has numerous legitimate bloodlines from Henry I, one of three spare sons of William the Bastard. Henry usurped the throne after possibly murdering his older brother William Rufus — a second foreshadowing of the feud between Harry and Prince William — and paid a heavy price when his only legitimate son drowned in the White Ship disaster in 1120. That resulted in the usurpation of royal spare Empress Matilda, plunging England into a bloody civil war known as The Anarchy.

Harry also descends from many of Henry I's two dozen illegitimate children with one bloodline from Henry FitzHenry through Henry Carey — an alleged illegitimate son of Henry VII's spare son Henry VIII — and another bloodline through Henrietta FitzJames, an illegitimate daughter of James II (the spare son of James I's spare son Charles I who was beheaded in 1649).

JAMES II, nicknamed the Beshitten, is central to the third layer of Prince Harry's curse because the future king's initials, DY for Duke of York, were branded on thousands of slaves transported across the Atlantic by the Royal African Company, possibly including some of Meghan Markle's ancestors. It is also possible that Harry descends from a branded slave on a Barbados plantation owned by an ancestor of Edward Lascelles, the first Earl of Harewood (who descended from Henry FitzHenry through an illegitimate daughter of the allegedly illegitimate Edward IV).

After slavery was banned throughout the British Empire in 1833, thousands of British slave owners — including a great-great-grandfather of Harry's 'Gan-Gan', the Queen Mother — were compensated by the British Government led by Harry's ancestor Earl Grey (after whom the tea was named). The total payout was billions of pounds in today's money, but the slaves got nothing and their ancestors are still waiting for an apology, let alone reparations.

Noah cursing Ham

HARRY descends from some of America's first slaveowners who believed that Africans were cursed through Noah's spare son Ham with black skin and servitude, hence marriages between whites and blacks were illegal So, if Harry's children Archie and Lilibet had been born before the American Civil War, they would have been cursed with illegitimacy as well as racism. (In late 2023, the senior royals who allegedly asked about the colour of Harry's first child were identified as Charles III and Kate, the Princess of Wales.)

Cain Killing Abel

THERE IS another slavery-related biblical story in the fourth layer of Harry's curse involving Adam's spare son Abel. He was killed by older brother Cain whose descendants were supposedly marked with dark skin (although some say the mark was red hair). Coincidentally, Harry and his brother have an extremely rare form of Indian DNA inherited through an all-female bloodline from Eliza Kewark, wife of Theodore Forbes who worked for the notorious East India Company. As depicted in the *Taboo* TV series, the EIC was involved in the slave trade, although mostly across the Indian Ocean.

(In line with the other layers in Harry's curse, at least seven of Theodore Forbes' great-grandparents descended from Henry FitzHenry; Forbes abandoned Eliza because of racial prejudice; their daughter Kitty had a faithful companion who may have been an African slave; and, like Harry, Kitty suffered rumours of illegitimacy.)

Besides his mitochondrial DNA, Prince Harry has two ongoing links with British imperialism. Firstly, by his own admission, he killed 25 suspected Taliban fighters during his two tours in Afghanistan and that resulted in an Islamic curse which threatens the safety of Harry and his family. Secondly, both India and Afghanistan have demanded that Britain return the famous Kohinoor diamond — wrongly described by Harry as the world's biggest — which has supposedly cursed the royals since 1851 when it was given to Queen Victoria. She transmitted haemophilia to at least ten of her descendants, including four offspring of Prince Henry of Battenberg (one of whom nearly died when he was circumcised.)

Queen Victoria may also have transmitted porphyria — which allegedly caused George III's madness — to Prince Henry's son Prince William of Gloucester (a grandson of royal spare George V and a nephew of royal spare George VI). William, after whom Harry's brother was named, died in a plane crash in 1972.

THE FIFTH layer in Harry's curse has a lot to do with his fourth given name (David) and a discredited doctrine known as British Israelism which has links to antisemitism and white supremacy. Underlying the doctrine are two beliefs: that the British people descend from the Ten Lost Tribes of Israel, and that members of the  royal family are lineal descendants of King David (above) — a mentally unstable murderer and adulterer who was probably illegitimate and red-haired — through David I of Scotland and his son Prince Henry.

After convincing himself that his marriage to Catherine of Aragon incurred a biblical curse, Henry VIII ruthlessly exploited King David's story in his quest for absolute power. Henry then became Defender of the Faith, a title now held by Harry's adulterous father. (Like the Jewish king, Charles III was circumcised soon after birth and, according to his memoir, so was Prince Harry.)

THE SIXTH layer in Harry's curse is his ginger hair which was obviously inherited from his Spencer ancestors. But, unfortunately for Harry, several of his mother's lovers (notably James Hewitt) also had red hair, fuelling rumours about his illegitimacy. Even more unfortunate was the 2015 plot by a redhead neo-Nazi to assassinate Prince Charles and Prince William so that Harry could be crowned Henry IX.

Britain has a long history of redheaded monarchs, starting with William the Bastard's son William Rufus. Henry II and several other Plantagenets had red hair and so did most of the Tudors, including Elizabeth I. It was a blessing for her, especially after Henry VIII declared her illegitimate, but for Prince Harry — who has admitted being bullied because of his hair colour — the 'ginger gene' is more like a curse which has now passed to his children.

ONE OF the best-known biblical redheads is Judas Iscariot (depicted above leaving the last supper) who was referenced by royal author Amanda Platell in the *Daily Mail* (January 2023). 'How could Harry so publicly shatter for ever those brotherly bonds after what they've been through,' Platell wrote. 'All to line the Sussexes' pockets with 30 pieces of Netflix silver.'

MENTAL illness is the final layer of Harry's curse, with a wide range of possible afflictions, including agoraphobia, attention deficit disorder, depression, paranoia, post-traumatic stress disorder, plus an Oedipus Complex thrown in for good measure. However, it could be a classic case of too much counselling. According to Prince William, Harry has been 'brainwashed by an army of therapists'.

There are several other curses hanging over Harry, including the Spencer curse which supposedly doomed Princess Diana. Understandably, Harry's biggest fear is that wife Meghan could suffer the same fate. In the meantime, Harry is busy committing 'brand suicide' and there is little chance that he will reconcile with the future William V (who views 'Harold' as 'a curse on the monarchy'). As Karl Marx reputedly said: 'History repeats itself, first as tragedy, second as farce.'

1

Prince Harry's Curse

The Curse of the Royal Spare

IN LATE 2023, as Prince Harry and Meghan Markle faced the possible loss of their royal titles, two British commentators disagreed on whether Charles III's self-exiled youngest son will ever get a glorious homecoming.

'The country would go out to welcome him,' said Tory MP Jacob Rees-Mogg, 'as long as he came back in the way the prodigal son did, with humility and asking the nation to take him back into their arms.' But Angela Levin disagreed. 'I think it would be very hard for him to get the nation to like him… because of what he said about his father, the lies he's told, I think he's remembered everything from a small age. William got one more sausage than him and he's very annoyed about it.'

Three years earlier, the editor of *Majesty* magazine speculated about Elizabeth II's attitude towards Harry. 'There's a story in the Bible about the prodigal son,' wrote Ingrid Seward, 'a boy who did everything wrong and then came back and his father accepted him… [The Queen] is always willing to forgive, she may not forget, but she is willing to forgive.'

The Return of the Prodigal Son

WHILE the biblical comparison is apt, no attention has been paid to the prodigal son's disgruntled brother. As Simcha Fisher wrote in *America Magazine* in 2017, the oldest son is the 'faithful one' who always does what his father asks. 'And then there is this young punk, his little brother, who is brought up in the same household but runs off and squanders everything… When he finally staggers home again (and is he truly contrite or mostly just hungry?) his father rejoices, puts a ring on his finger, slaughters a fatted calf. The elder brother is mad and hurt… How is this right?'

PRINCE HARRY has hated the Bible since a teacher hit him with a hardcover edition at Eton, so he will almost certainly disregard the prodigal son story. However, he could learn a great deal by studying previous royal spares, especially his disgraced uncle Prince Andrew and outrageous great-aunt Princess Margaret, and also the last two King Georges.

In *The Crown* TV series, Prince Philip's character propounded a fictional theory reminiscent of some famous royal curses: 'There have always been the dazzling Windsors and the dull ones'. It started with Edward VII's scandal-plagued oldest son Prince Albert Victor whose death in 1892 may have been caused by a coronavirus. Albert Victor outshone his stamp-collecting younger brother, the future George V; and Nazi sympathiser Edward VIII (known to family and friends as David) totally eclipsed the future George VI (whose real first name was Albert).

SHORTLY before his death, George V predicted Edward's ruin and prayed to God that nothing would come between 'Bertie and Lilibet and the throne'. As depicted in *The King's Speech,* George VI's painful transition from spare to monarch was made worse by the cruelty of his father and his brother's mockery. But, with the help of unauthodox Australian therapist Lionel Logue, Bertie became an inspiring leader during World War II and was widely mourned when he died in 1952 aged just 56.

The next dull Windsor was Prince Philip's wife Elizabeth II who was famously steadfast and reserved compared to her glamorous sibling. 'When my sister and I were growing up, she was made out to be the goody-goody one,' Margaret explained. 'That was boring, so the press tried to make out that I was as wicked as hell.'

IN HIS 2023 memoir, Harry describes 'Aunt Margo' as almost a total stranger. 'Like most Britons, I mainly knew *of* her. I was conversant with the general contours of her sad life. Great loves thwarted by the Palace. Exuberant streaks of self-destruction splashed across the tabloids.'

'Her relationship with Granny wasn't an exact analogue of mine

Princess Margaret died in 2002 shortly before the Queen Mother.

with Willy, but pretty close,' Harry wrote. 'The simmering rivalry, the intense competition.' It all looked familiar, especially when Harry had to ask for permission to marry Meghan Markle. The worst-case scenario was the Queen saying no, dooming him to be the 'next Margaret'.

Prince Andrew and Prince Charles have never been close, which is not surprising given their different personalities and the 12-year age gap, but their relationship reached breaking point in the early 1990s when Charles — with his popularity plummeting after divorcing Diana — suspected family members were plotting to oust him as heir. According to Nigel Cawthorne, author of *Windsor Spares: The Prince Harry and Prince Andrew Soap Opera* (2023), Charles feared that Prince William could succeed Elizabeth II with the egotistical Andrew serving as regent until William turned 18.

THIRTY YEARS later, following the Epstein scandal, Andrew was facing eviction from Royal Lodge at Windsor and there was speculation he could be stripped of his remaining titles. So, hypothetically, Harry could become Duke of York - the title traditionally given to a monarch's second son — with a bastard bloodline from a previous Duke of York (James II) whose initials may have been branded on slave ancestors of Harry's children.

Like Prince Andrew, Harry found refuge in the military. And because 'the spare could always be spared' he was allowed to serve in Afghanistan, flying helicopters just as his uncle had done during the Falklands War in 1982. There was a big downside for Harry, because frontline service triggered trauma from his mother's death, but he found 'a sort of cure' after creating the Invictus Games.

In September 2021, Harry's future looked bright. 'Now a comfortable sixth in line to the throne, [he] has forged his own path, looking for a life not dominated by his status as the second son… he may finally have broken the curse of the spare, while his uncle Andrew's life lies in tatters,' wrote Hadley Hall Meares in a *Vanity Fair* article titled 'The Tortured History of the Royal Spare'.

BUT LESS than eighteen months later, it was painful to watch Harry committing 'brand suicide'. Thanks to *Spare*, he had become Britain's second most unpopular royal (after Prince Andrew). 'Even younger audiences, who generally held kinder views of Prince Harry, are turning against him. And the media sentiment in the USA seems to be following suit,' wrote Jeetendr Sehdev in *Forbes* magazine (January 2023).

While Charles III will probably forgive Harry, it is less likely that Prince William will do the same, especially after Harry wrote about the fight they had in 2019. 'It all happened so fast,' Harry wrote. 'He grabbed me by the collar, ripping my necklace, and he knocked me to the floor. I landed on the dog's bowl, which cracked under my back, the pieces cutting into me. I lay there for a moment, dazed, then got to my feet and told him to get out.' As William was leaving, he advised Harry not to tell Meghan. 'You mean that you attacked me?' asked Harry, to which William responded: 'I didn't attack you, Harold.'

2

Prince Harry's Curse

House of the Dragon

GIVEN that Harold is Prince William's nickname for Harry, and that William's naval nickname was 'Dragon', it is worth noting that the English king killed in 1066 was a noble spare who, like William the Bastard, had dragon connections. Note also that Harry and William descend from both kings through spare sons of Edward III, whose patron saint was the dragon-slaying St George.

Harold Godwinson's older brother Sweyn, who claimed to be a son (presumably illegitimate) of King Canute, was exiled after murdering his cousin and died on a barefoot pilgrimage to Jerusalem. That left Harold as heir to the Earl of Wessex and ultimately first in line to succeed Aethelred the Unready's spare son Edward the Confessor as

England's rightful king, regardless of any promise made to William the Bastard.

The Bastard's victory supposedly fulfilled a Merlin prophecy that the fire-breathing 'Dark Dragon' of Normandy would defeat the white dragon of England and then 'burn up the entire island', an apparent reference to the infamous Harrying of the North which began in 1069, about one year after the birth of Henry I.

AS DEPICTED in the Bayeux Tapestry, King Harold flew the Wessex dragon banner — previously flown by Aethelwulf's spare son Alfred the Great — which was later adopted by Henry II's spare son Richard the Lionheart. In the meantime, England suffered two decades of anarchy which inspired the *Game of Thrones* prequel *House of the Dragon*. The TV series features King Viserys (based on Henry I) and his dragon-riding daughter Rhaenyra (Empress Matilda) who ends up marrying her father's younger brother Daemon Targaryen. Daemon was played by Matt Smith who also played Prince Philip in *The Crown* TV series, which explains why Harry called Matt 'Grandad' when they first met.

Comparisons between Prince Harry and Daemon Targaryen were inevitable because they are both 'volatile and impulsive' royal spares. 'You know you've hit rock bottom when compared to a fictional character,' wrote Cassandra Hawkings on the Project Fangirl website. 'Daemon tries to set up his own royal court, just as Harry is attempting in the United States. He throws a temper tantrum when he doesn't get his own way and mutilates a dude's face with his pointy-as-hell helmet.'

HARRY has compared himself to another royal spare in *Game of Thrones*, Daenerys Targaryen (partly based on Henry VII) who descended from Aegon the Conqueror (obviously inspired by

William the Bastard). Daenerys unwittingly sleeps with her allegedly illegitimate nephew Jon Snow (real name Aegon Targaryen), one of several candidates for the Jesus-inspired Prince Who Was Promised who wielded a sword reminiscent of King Arthur's Excalibur.

Daenerys Targaryen is supported by a 'rowdy, rough-and-tumble private army' known as the Second Sons. According to the Fandom website: 'The name of the company comes from the tradition of firstborn children in noble or wealthy families receiving inheritance, property and titles from their parents, while second sons receive nothing. Second sons (and younger) therefore often seek their fortunes in the wider world by joining sellsword companies.'

Vlad the Impaler

JON SNOW'S illegitimate arch-rival Ramsay Bolton — who enjoys skinning his victims alive — has been compared to Vlad the Impaler, from whom Prince Harry descends through George V's wife Mary of Teck, previously the fiancé of George's deceased brother Prince Albert Victor. Harry knows all about Vlad — the second son of his namesake father who inspired the fictional Dracula — because Charles III owns properties in Romania where he is unofficially known as the Prince of Transylvania.

Some say a curse laid by Vlad the Impaler, which threatened an afterlife with the biblical Judas, caused a plague which killed about half the population of Romania's capital city Bucharest in the early 1800s.

VLAD THE IMPALER was a member of the Order of the Dragon (insignia right) which was co-founded in 1408 by alleged lesbian vampire Barbara of Cilli and Sigismund of Bohemia. Sigismund visited Henry V in London where he joined the Order of the Garter founded by Edward III in 1348. Both orders venerated the dragon-slaying St George who reputedly inspired Richard I during the Third Crusade.

For Henry III, unfurling of the dragon banner meant no mercy to his enemies; Edward I flew a red dragon banner while he was hammering the Scots; and Henry V had a dragon banner at Agincourt where, according to Shakespeare, he delivered the immortal words: 'Cry God for Harry, England, and Saint George!'

LIKE his father-in-law and fellow usurper Edward IV, Henry VII (pictured left with his wife and children, including Henry VIII) exploited the legend of St George to bolster his claim to the throne, and he also incorporated the red dragon of Wales into his coat of arms. Charles II was depicted as St George killing a dragon; so was George III, in several satirical cartoons; and in early 2024, to celebrate the Chinese Year of the Dragon, the Royal Mint released a Charles III gold coin with an image of St George on the reverse.

EDWARD VII's spare son George V was very proud of the dragon tattoo which he got in Japan in 1881. Prince Philip's uncle (and royal spare) Prince George of Greece had a similar tattoo, and it would not be surprising if Harry's nephew, the current Prince George, does the same because one of his favourite films is *How to Train Your Dragon*.

In 2018, Harry married Meghan Markle at Windsor Castle in St George's Chapel, the spiritual home of the Order of the Garter. As the monarch's second son, Harry would normally be a member by now but he forwent the honour after stepping back from royal duties in 2020. Elizabeth II's disgraced spare son Prince Andrew, who has been a Garter Knight since 2006, was banned from the order's annual procession in 2022 and 2023.

AFTER winning a court battle against the *Mirror* newspaper in 2023, Harry issued a brief statement: 'I've been told that slaying dragons will get you burned, but in light of today's victory and the importance of doing what is needed for a free and honest press, it is a worthwhile price to pay. The mission continues.'

(*Note:* There are dragon-like creatures in the Bible, including a 'leviathan' described in the Book of Job: 'His snorting throws out flashes of light; his eyes are like the rays of dawn. Firebrands stream from his mouth; sparks of fire shoot out. Smoke pours from his nostrils as from a boiling pot over a fire of reeds. His breath sets coals ablaze, and flames dart from his mouth. Strength resides in his neck; dismay goes before him.')

3

Sins of the Father

Prince Harry's Curse

MERLIN'S prophecy referring to William the Bastard as the Dark Dragon of Normandy includes this biblical-sounding passage: 'Because of the sins of the father, the sons will sin against the father, and the sin that was first will be the cause of the sins that follow. The sons will rise against the father and the bowels will conspire about the belly in revenge… blood will rise and the strife will be terrible.'

William the Bastard's biggest 'sin', the genocidal Harrying of the North, resulted in him being cursed by the Archbishop of York. Ten years later, in 1079, the Bastard cursed his rebellious oldest son Robert Curthose after he unhorsed his father in battle. And finally, in 1087, the enormously fat king died after the pommel of his saddle was driven into his intestines. Merlin's prophecy was fulfilled when the Bastard's corpse exploded during his funeral.

COINCIDENTALLY, two of William the Bastard's sons, and one of his grandsons, all died while hunting in the New Forest. Richard of Normandy, Britain's first royal spare, died around 1070 aged about 16; his younger brother William Rufus (above) died thirty years later; and an illegitimate son of Robert Curthose died somewhere in the forest in the same year. Richard of Normandy was the first of many royal spares to die young, including the offspring of four King Henrys and three King Edwards.

Prince Harry descends from about half of the two dozen bastards of William Rufus's younger brother Henry I whose surname, Beauclerc, meant good scholar. Henry feuded with the red-haired, fiery-tempered William while Robert Curthose was crusading in the Holy Land.

In the sixth season of *The Crown* TV series, Prince Harry tells the future William V that William II was 'assassinated by his brother'. Harry explains how his namesake killed William's namesake in a hunting 'accident' and then galloped off to Winchester to claim the throne. 'Don't worry, mate,' says Harry reassuringly, 'I wouldn't do that to you.'

Interestingly, because he was born after William the Bastard was crowned in 1066, Henry I claimed he had a greater claim to the throne than Robert Curthose who was born around 1051. Based on this theory, known as porphyrogeniture or 'born in the purple', the disgraced Prince Andrew (born 1960) is Britain's rightful king because Charles III was born four years before Elizabeth II became queen in 1952.

 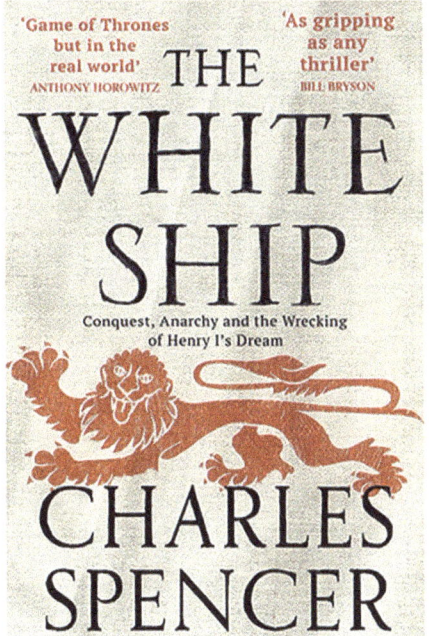

HARRY'S uncle Charles Spencer knows a great deal about Henry I and his only legitimate son, William Adelin, who drowned in the White Ship disaster of 1120. Spencer helped find the wreck in shallow waters off the French coast in 2021 and subsequently wrote *The White Ship: Conquest, Anarchy and the Wrecking of Henry I's Dream.* According to Anthony Horowitz, it is *'Game of Thrones* but in the real world'.

In keeping with the biblical theme of this book, it is worth noting the words of one chronicler about King Henry's grief after the death of his oldest son: 'Not Jacob was more woe-stricken for the loss of Joseph, nor did David give vent to more woeful lamentations for the murder of Ammon or Absalom.'

AFTER the death of William Adelin, Henry I had only one legitimate heir, the Empress Matilda (left), who was Britain's first female royal spare. Matilda had a maternal bloodline from the House of Wessex and most of the barons swore solemn oaths to Henry I that they would support her. However, there was widespread opposition to a female ruler and that enabled Matilda's first cousin Stephen of Blois to seize the throne, resulting in nearly twenty years of bloodshed known as The Anarchy.

When King Stephen died in 1154 his spare son William of Blois could have been crowned William III but, for the sake of peace, he supported his second cousin who became Henry II. William died childless in 1159 aged about 22, and Henry's younger brother William FitzEmpress died five years later aged 27 (suggesting a possible curse on Prince William's royal namesakes).

LIKE William Rufus, Henry II was a temperamental redhead and it is not surprising that he fought continuously with his four surviving sons: Henry the Young King, whose older brother William died in infancy; Richard the Lionheart, of Robin Hood fame; Geoffrey, Duke of Brittany; and King John, best known for signing Magna Carta. In *The Lion in Winter* (1968), set after the death of his namesake son, Henry II blames everyone but himself:

'My life, when it is written, will read better than it lived… Henry FitzEmpress, first Plantagenet, a king at twenty-one, the ablest soldier of an able time. He led men well, he cared for justice when he could and ruled, for thirty years, a state as great as Charlemagne's. He married out of love, a woman out of legend… She bore him many children. But no sons. King Henry had no sons. He had three whiskered things but he disowned them.' Henry then wishes plague on his sons and hopes that all their children 'breech and die'.

WHILE Henry II never said the most famous words attributed to him: 'Will no-one rid me of this turbulent priest?' he was not entirely blameless for the *Game of Thrones*-style murder of Thomas Becket in Canterbury Cathedral. Ultimately, as Merlin had supposedly predicted, Henry was punished by his own offspring, with the notable exception of Geoffrey the Bastard who was the only son at the king's deathbed in 1189. (According to some sources, Prince Harry descends from one of Becket's murderers, William de Tracy, whose namesake father was a bastard son of Henry I.)

HISTORY has been astonishingly kind to Henry II's spare son Richard the Lionheart (inset) who, according to renowned scholar William Stubbs, was 'a bad son, a bad husband, a selfish ruler, and a vicious man'. Depicted left are some of the 3000 men, women and children massacred by the Lionheart at Ayyadieh, largely because Saladin refused to hand over a piece of the True Cross (two splinters of which were given to Charles III before his coronation).

IN 2011, when a terrorist group condemned Prince Harry for fighting in Afghanistan, it was widely accepted that Muslims have bitter memories about the crusades inherited from their medieval ancestors. But, according to Cambridge historian Jonathan Riley Smith, 'nothing could be further from the truth [because] it is only a slight exaggeration to say that between 1500 and 1860 the most original writings on the Crusades in Arabic were nostalgic about them.' Professor Paul F Crawford concurred in a 2011 article. 'It was not the crusades that taught Islam to attack and hate Christians,' he wrote, 'it was the West which taught Islam to hate the crusades. The irony is rich.'

WHEN Richard the Lionheart died from a crossbow wound in 1199, he was succeeded by his youngest brother King John even though the rightful heir was their teenaged nephew Arthur (left), son of Henry II's fourth son Geoffrey (not to be confused with his half-brother Geoffrey the Bastard). After Arthur's presumed murder in 1203, his sister — who should have been crowned Queen Eleanor— was held captive for nearly 40 years, firstly by King John and then by Henry III.

15

4

Prince Harry's Curse

Descended from the Devil

LIKE Henry II's rebellious son Richard I, Prince Harry is a red-headed royal spare who has been cursed for killing Muslims. And, like the Lionheart, Harry has the dubious distinction of being descended from the Devil's daughter (who probably inspired the Starbucks mermaid).

Harry's accursedness was painfully obvious on the day that he was born when Prince Charles congratulated himself for having produced 'an heir and a spare'. But Charles' initial response to baby Harry was even more insensitive: 'Oh God, it's a boy. And he's even got red hair.'

Diana knew that she was expecting a boy but never told Charles because he had his heart set on a girl, a reversal of Diana's birth when her parents wanted a boy. Gender preference is inherently unfair and so is 'gingerism', a relatively new term for prejudice against red-headed people. Harry has been bullied because of his hair colour and knows the same fate awaits Archie and Lilibet who have inherited his 'ginger gene'.

The Fallen Angel by Alexandre Cabanel

THE DEVIL, also known as Satan or Lucifer 'the fallen angel', has often been depicted with red hair and there is another tradition of red-headed people being called 'the Devil's spawn'. Prince Harry probably knew some of this while training with the elite Red Devils parachute regiment.

Richard the Lionheart famously joked about his family's demonic heritage through the House of Anjou: 'From the Devil we came, and to the Devil we shall go'. It was a reference to Melusine, the mythical ancestress of the Plantagenets — and countless millions of people with English heritage — through the husband of Empress Matilda. Henry VIII descended from a different version of Melusine through his maternal great-grandmother Jacquetta of Luxembourg, and from yet another version through the Lusignan ancestors of Edward IV's mother Cecily Neville.

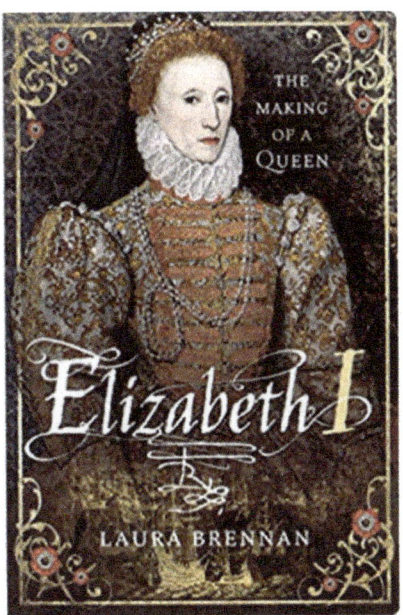 

PRINCE HARRY has multiple Melusine bloodlines through red-headed Mary Queen of Scots, nicknamed 'Fair Devil', who was executed by her red-headed first cousin once removed Elizabeth I. Mary became heir to the throne after her two older brothers died in infancy. And Elizabeth, whose mother Anne Boleyn was falsely accused of having 'marks of the devil' (including six fingers on one hand), became queen after the deaths of her half-brother Edward VI and her half-sister Bloody Mary. Elizabeth and Mary both died childless (See next chapter).

The legendary Melusine

AS SHOWN above, Melusine's husband was shocked to discover that she was a serpent in disguise. According to one legend, Melusine was a daughter of the King of Scotland and grew up on the island of Avalon which has connections to King Arthur. In northern France, there is another legend about Melusine transforming into a flying dragon and building a huge chateau near Poitiers in just fifteen days. And in Luxembourg, Melusine lived in a castle on the Bock promontory.

Melusine inspired the *Game of Thrones* character Melisandre, known as the Red Witch because of her burgundy-coloured hair, and also the Starbucks mermaid who was depicted with red hair on packets of the 2015 anniversary blend.

The Princes in the Tower

IN PHILIPPA GREGORY'S novel *The King's Curse* (2014), Edward IV's wife Elizabeth Woodville and their daughter Elizabeth of York (who both had red hair) ask Melusine to curse whoever killed the older Elizabeth's sons: Edward V and his brother Richard, Duke of York (the Princes in the Tower). The request is very specific: 'Whoever took our firstborn son, you will take his firstborn son from him, and his grandsons too, and his firstborn boys all down his line. And we will know the murderer by the workings of our curse.'

Richard of York's spare son Richard III appears to have been the main victim, reputedly killed by Prince Harry's poleaxe-wielding ancestor Rhys ap Thomas one year after the mysterious death of Richard III's only legitimate son, Edward of Middleham. But thereafter the curse fell on Elizabeth Woodville's own descendants, including Henry VII's firstborn son Prince Arthur, who died aged 15 in 1502, plus three of Henry VII's firstborn grandsons who all died in infancy: Henry VIII's son Henry Cornwall, Mary Tudor's son Henry Brandon, and Margaret Tudor's son James, Earl of Rothesay.

As Philippa Langley revealed in a TV program in 2023, there is compelling evidence that Edward IV's spare son Richard escaped death in the Tower of London and tried to claim the throne as Perkin Warbeck (right). Mary Shelley, whose Gothic novel *Frankenstein* was inspired by the character of Satan in Milton's *Paradise Lost,* reached the same conclusion about Warbeck in a book published in 1830.

Henry VIII's illegitimate son Henry Fitzroy — who could conceivably have become Henry IX — died in 1536 aged 17, possibly a victim of cystic fibrosis (an inherited disease similar to tuberculosis). Either way, as Kyra Kramer points out in *Edward IV in a Nutshell,* Edward and his half-brother Fitzroy, and also Henry VIII's older brother Arthur, all died with similar symptoms. And, based on an old saying, there is no doubt that cystic fibrosis was considered a curse: 'Woe to the child who tastes salty from a kiss on the brow, for he is cursed and soon will die.'

In support of her fictional curse, Philippa Gregory cited Kyra Kramer's theory that Henry VIII had the rare Kell positive blood type which can kill babies when the mother is Kell negative. In other words, the inability of Henry VIII's wives to produce a male heir may have resulted from blood that he inherited from Jacquetta of Luxembourg (whose family allegedly descended from Melusine) through Elizabeth Woodville and Elizabeth of York. Bad blood would also explain Henry VIII's worsening behaviour which was consistent with the Kell-related McLeod syndrome.

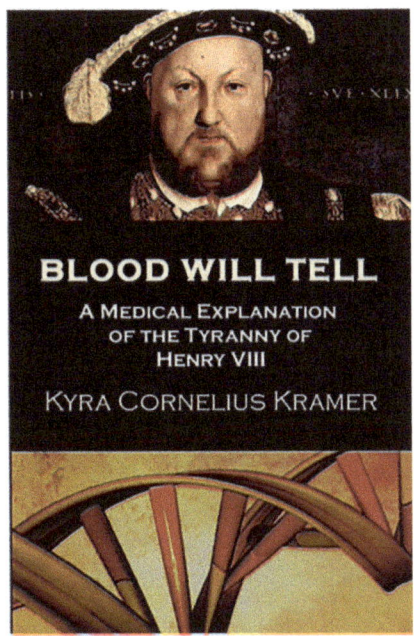

A 1530s mural of Henry VIII discovered in a former rectory in Milverton, Somerset, in 2011 is noteworthy because, when viewed upside down, the king's features transform into a terrifying image of the devil.

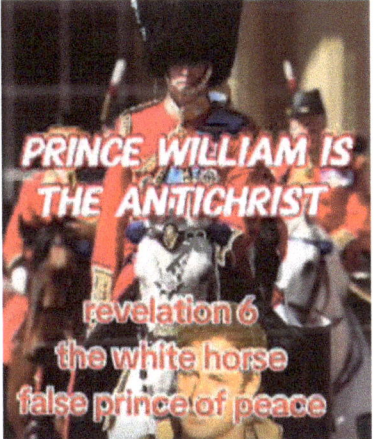

Photos: (left) Facebook; (right) TikTok

AT THE launch of the 2017 Invictus Games in Canada, Prince Harry allegedly made 'the sign of the devil' while standing next to Melania Trump. Some said the gesture was to ward off evil spirits, and others speculated about Harry being the Antichrist. Obviously, that was 'fake news' because, as shown above, Harry's brother has been outed on TikTok.

Meanwhile, on Reddit, Harry's coat of arms has been linked to bible passages about the Antichrist's white horse and a leopard-like beast with the face of a lion and the feet of a bear. The lions passant, known as 'the three cats, were adopted by Richard the Lionheart — based on arms attributed to William the Bastard, son of Robert the Devil — and the lion rampant represents William the Lion of Scotland (from whom Harry descends through three illegitimate daughters).

5  'They shall be childless'

Prince Harry's Curse

ANYONE who doubts that Prince Harry's royal ancestors were well and truly cursed should consider the sixteen monarchs between Henry V and George I, half of whom were spares. Incredibly, disregarding any known bastards, all of these monarchs either died childless or else their firstborn sons died childless.

Henry IV deserves much of the blame because, as royal blogger Rebecca Starr Brown has pointed out, the usurpation of Richard II's crown in 1399 was 'an unnatural crime against the very function of a succession and monarchy [that] would continue to undermine the House of Lancaster to varying degrees through the reign of Henry's son, Henry V, and his grandson, Henry VI. Finally, it would rear its head in the Wars of the Roses.'

It seems that Henry V and his son were victims of a famous 'prophecy': 'Henry born at Monmouth shall small time reign and much get, but Henry born at Windsor shall long reign and lose all.' The hero of Agincourt did die relatively young in 1422, and the mentally unstable Henry VI was allegedly murdered nearly fifty years later on the orders of his usurper Edward IV (who had a short-lived older brother named Henry).

HENRY VI's only child Edward of Westminster — who was possibly sired by Prince Harry's ancestor Edmund Beaufort — is depicted above being murdered in front of red-capped Edward IV and two of his brothers, the future Richard III (left) and George, Duke of Clarence (who was allegedly drowned in a vat of wine). Joffrey Baratheon, the most despicable bastard in *Game of Thrones,* was inspired by Edward of Westminster; Tyrion Lannister has a lot in common with Richard III; and Robb Stark resembles Edward IV.

As mentioned in the previous chapter, the presumed murder of the Princes in the Tower (Edward V and his brother Richard) inspired Philippa Gregory's 'King's Curse' which doomed the firstborn legitimate sons of usurpers Richard III and Henry VII, and also Henry VIII.

THE MARRIAGE of Henry VIII and Catherine of Aragon (above) was supposedly cursed because of a Bible passage: 'If a man shall take his brother's wife, it is an unclean thing… they shall be childless.' (Leviticus 20:21). Catherine delivered a daughter, the future Mary I, but Henry was determined to have a male heir. He used the biblical curse as an excuse to divorce Catherine, previously married to his older brother Arthur, and then married Anne Boleyn, the younger sister of Henry's former mistress Mary.

Cardinal Reginald Pole, a great-nephew of Edward IV and Richard III, wrote a scathing letter about Henry VIII's hypocrisy: 'Are you ignorant of the law which certainly no less prohibits marriage with a sister of one with whom you have become one flesh, than with one with whom your brother was one flesh?'

The Execution of Lady Jane Grey, by Paul Delaroche

EDWARD VI, who died aged 15, removed his half-sisters Mary and Elizabeth from the line of succession, claiming both had been rendered illegitimate by Henry VIII, and the next monarch was Lady Jane Grey (who had an older brother named Henry who died young). The redheaded teenager, who famously ruled for only nine days, was beheaded at the Tower of London in 1554. Mary I, a Catholic nicknamed Bloody Mary, died childless and so did the Protestant Elizabeth I who prided herself on being the Virgin Queen. Thus ended the Tudor dynasty.

The execution of Charles I

THE EARLY death of James I's firstborn son Prince Henry Frederick paved the way for Britain's most accursed royal spare, Charles I. Like George V's spare son George VI, Charles had a speech impediment, but his biggest fault was stubborn adherence to the divine right of kings. That resulted in a bloody civil war and his beheading in 1649, twenty years after his firstborn son (also named Charles) lived for just one day.

Charles I's second son, Charles II, had a dozen or so bastards (including two ancestors of Prince Harry) but his marriage to Catherine of Braganza was childless. Meanwhile, Charles Stuart, the firstborn son of the future James II, died aged six months in 1661, shortly after being made Duke of Cambridge. Remarkably, three other sons of James II died young with the same title (obviously a bad omen for Prince Harry's brother).

The Catholic James II was overthrown by Protestant William of Orange in the bloodless Glorious Revolution of 1688. Then, in a classic case of history repeating, the Stuart dynasty ended after James II's spare daughters, Mary II and Queen Anne, both died at Kensington Palace without any surviving children.

Jacobites claimed the death of 32-year-old Mary II from smallpox was divine retribution because she breached the fifth commandment: 'Honour thy father'. And Anne's death in 1714 fulfilled a famous prophecy about the Stuarts whose royal bloodline started with one of Robert the Bruce's daughters almost exactly 400 years earlier: 'It came with a lass, and it will go with a lass'.

QUEEN ANNE suffered more than any other female spare because, after at least 17 pregnancies, her only child was Prince William, Duke of Gloucester. He died in 1700, aged 11, after spending some of his childhood in the allegedly cursed Kensington Palace (above) where the current Prince William and Harry lived with Princess Diana. Queen

Victoria had a miserable childhood under the so-called Kensington System imposed by her mother's alleged lover, and Princess Margaret lived in the palace after her messy divorce from Lord Snowdon. Altogether, at least seven princesses associated with the palace were either 'sad, bad or even mad'.

George I and James Francis Edward Stuart, the Old Pretender

WHILE the curse of the royal spare continued, the incredible 300-year sequence of royal childlessness ended in 1714 when an obscure German 'elector' named George Ludwig became King of England ahead of more than fifty Catholics, most notably James II's only surviving son who claimed he was James III. The Old Pretender's childless spare son Cardinal Henry Benedict Stuart, younger brother of Bonnie Prince Charlie, was one of many hypothetical Henry IXs (See Chapter 17).

Another childless royal spare was George III's second son Prince Frederick who is best remembered for the nursery rhyme about ten thousand men marching up and down a hill. There have been numerous parodies, including one about Elizabeth II's spare son Prince Andrew which appeared in early 2022:

'The grand old Duke of York, he had twelve million quid / He gave it to someone he never met, for something he never did.'

NOT SURPRISINGLY, Prince Harry has expressed concern about the current royal spare, his niece Princess Charlotte, who has a special place in royal history because she wasn't displaced when Prince Louis was born in 2018. Harry told the *Daily Telegraph:* 'Though William and I have talked about it once or twice, and he has made it very clear to me that his kids are not my responsibility, I still feel a responsibility knowing that out of those three children, at least one will end up like me, the spare.'

The bad news for Louis is that his cheekiness is reminiscent of young Harry. So the curse which began with the second son of William the Bastard has seemingly fallen on the second son of the future William V.

6

Badges of Bastardy

UNFORTUNATELY for Prince Harry, the Mountbatten and Windsor surnames he was born with had previously been 'badges of bastardy', and his new Sussex surname is also linked to illegitimacy. The inclusion of Meghan Markle's coat of arms on sussex.com has made things even worse, and history suggests that could be a bad omen for Prince Archie and Princess Lilibet.

In late 1959, shortly before Elizabeth II gave birth to her spare son Prince Andrew, a meddlesome lawyer named Edward Iwi made a sensational claim: If the baby was surnamed Windsor it would be a 'badge of bastardy' because only illegitimate children were named after their mothers.

Prince Charles and Princess Anne, born in 1948 and 1950, had been surnamed Mountbatten — which, ironically, was Prince Philip's mother's name — but, after his wife assumed the throne in 1952, it was decreed that any future children would be Windsors. Prince Philip bitterly complained he was the only man in Britain whose children could not inherit his surname. 'I'm just a bloody amoeba,' he said.

After the 'badge of bastardy' bombshell, it was quickly decided that the Queen's second son, and future male-line descendants, would be Mountbatten-Windsors. That surname wasn't on Prince Harry's marriage certificate, because technically he does not have a surname, but it was on the birth certificates of his children, Archie and Lilibet.

August de Grancy, Prince Alexander and Julia Hauke

MOUNTBATTEN is the Anglicised form of Battenberg, a noble title created out of thin air for Julia Hauke, the daughter of a Polish general who (like Meghan Markle) was socially inferior to her husband, Prince Alexander of Hesse and by Rhine, who (like Prince Harry) was rumoured to be illegitimate. In fact, Alexander was almost certainly sired by a Swiss stablemaster named August von Senarclens de Grancy and is most likely the first royal bastard from whom Prince Harry descends.

Prince Louis of Battenberg's 'badge of bastardy'

BECAUSE the marriage of Prince Alexander and Julia Hauke was morganatic, even though she became Princess of Battenberg, none of their children could inherit the Hesse title or name. That explains why Prince Philip's grandfather was born Louis, Prince of Battenberg, and why his coat of arms — which quartered the rampant lion of the House of Hesse and the black and white stripes of Battenberg — is definitely a 'badge of bastardy'.

(Prince Louis, not to be confused with his nephew Lord Louis Mountbatten, allegedly fathered an illegitimate daughter by actress Lillie Langtry who, like Queen Camilla's ancestor Alice Keppel, was one of Edward VII's mistresses.)

PRINCE PHILIP'S real surname was Glucksburg, the dynastic name of his father Prince Andrew of Greece and Denmark who abandoned his children and lived with his mistress, a fake countess who spent nearly all of Philip's inheritance. So, unsurprisingly, Philip preferred the maiden name of his mother, Princess Alice, who died in 1969. As shown right, Philip's arms included the black and white stripes of Battenberg inherited from Julia Hauke and 'a representation of Hercules girt about the loins with a lion skin'. Weirdly inappropriate but perfectly suited for the gaffe-prone Duke of Edinburgh.

Prince Philip's coat of arms

(While Philip fought valiantly for Britain during World War II, he had four Nazi-sympathising brothers-in-law, including two named Hesse, who would have got on well with the traitorous Edward VIII.)

THE CHANGE from Battenberg to Mountbatten coincided with the 1917 decision by George V (left) — forced on the king by anti-German sentiment during World War I — to rebrand the House of Saxe-Coburg and Gotha as the House of Windsor. As revealed in the *Victoria* TV series, George V's grandfather Prince Albert may have been sired by his uncle Leopold. Either way, Prince Harry descends from two German princes who, like him, were rumoured to be illegitimate. The main difference with Prince Albert of Saxe-Coburg and Gotha is that he was socially inferior to his wife.

Henry Fitzroy and his bend sinister

IRONICALLY, Prince Harry has been more afflicted by the curse of illegitimacy than many of the royal bastards from whom he descends, most notably two sons of Charles II: Henry Fitzroy, the first Duke of Grafton; and Charles Lennox, the first Duke of Richmond. They did very well for themselves and so did four of their half-brothers who were also dukes.

The bend sinister on Henry Fitzroy's arms did signify illegitimacy but that was not always the case. And there is a similar misconception about the Fitz prefix. Many royal bastards in Harry's family tree can be easily identified by the surname Fitzroy ('son of the king'), or specific names such as FitzHenry and FitzJames, but Harry also descends from totally legitimate FitzGeralds, FitzMaurices, FitzWalters and so on.

John 'Fairborn' Beaufort and his bend dexter

THROUGH illegitimate offspring of Charles II, James II, Henry VIII and Edward IV, Prince Harry has bloodlines from John Beaufort, the oldest bastard son of John of Gaunt and the socially inferior Katherine Swynford. John Junior, ironically nicknamed 'Fairborn', declared his illegitimacy with a bend dexter. Gaunt's legitimate son, Henry IV, barred the Beauforts from claiming the throne, even after they were twice legitimated, echoing a prophecy that Shakespeare used in Macbeth: 'Thou shalt beget kings even though thou be none.'

Henry VII's mother Margaret was a granddaughter of John 'Fairborn' Beaufort and it is entirely possible that Henry's father, Edmund Tudor, was actually sired by Margaret's first cousin Edmund Beaufort, who had a well-documented affair with Henry V's widow Catherine of Valois before she slept with the socially inferior Owen Tudor. (Young Edmund was illegitimate either way because Owen's marriage to Queen Catherine was illegal.)

PRINCE HARRY has Tudor bloodlines through George I whose longtime mistress, Melusine von der Schulenburg (right), delivered their namesake illegitimate daughter in 1693, one year before George allegedly murdered his wife's lover and then imprisoned her for the next 30 years (also banning her from seeing the future George II). Melusine, named after the legendary 'daughter of Satan' who spawned the Plantagenets, was made Duchess of Kendal with her own coat of arms.

As reported by the *Daily Mail* in 2018, Harry has a lot in common with George III's sixth son, Prince Augustus Frederick, who lived at Kensington Palace, spent time in exile; and was renowned for his liberal views. Augustus married Lady Augusta Murray in 1793 without the king's permission. That meant Augusta never became Duchess of Sussex but that didn't stop her from using the title to make money. The first duke's illegitimate children, Augustus (who had multiple sclerosis) and Augusta, were surnamed d'Este.

Harry and Meghan's 2024 rebrand was widely criticised because it made no mention of the royal family. And, by changing their children's surname from Mountbatten-Windsor to Sussex, the controversial couple caused Prince Philip to 'roll in his grave'.

The inclusion of Meghan's royal crest on sussex.com was hugely insensitive and also breached Elizabeth II's directive that the Sussexes should not profit from their royal titles. Time will tell if Charles III strips his spare son of his dukedom which, presumably, would force Harry to give Archie and Lilibet yet another surname. Wales, perhaps? Markle, of course, would be a 'badge of bastardy'.

7

Prince Harry's Curse

The Masque of Blackness

EVERYONE familiar with the 'colourblind' *Bridgerton* TV series will be surprised to learn that the only British queen who had a black face (albeit briefly) was James I's wife Anne of Denmark, and not George III's wife Queen Charlotte who supposedly descended from the illegitimate son of a Portuguese king and his Moorish mistress.

Queen Anne and six other white female ancestors of Prince Harry — including the countesses of Bedford, Derby and Suffolk — donned blackface makeup to portray African goddesses in *The Masque of Blackness* at Whitehall Palace on Twelfth Night (6th January) in 1605, the same day that James I's spare son, the future Charles I, became Duke of York.

Queen Anne and a black-faced masquer

The masque, written by renowned poet and playwright Ben Jonson, involves twelve daughters of the god Niger who are shocked to discover that blackness is unattractive. They end up in Britannia where its 'sun-like king' (James I) can bleach their black complexions white. According to Professor Bernadette Andrea from the University of California, the masque reveals 'complicity with an emerging institutional racism as England's increasing investment in the transatlantic slave trade underwrote its imperialist expansion into the Americas'.

In her 2018 animated film *The Masque of Blackness,* Epoh Beech weaved together elements of Ben Jonson's play and Joseph Conrad's *Heart of Darkness,* famously described by Nigerian novelist Chinua Achebe as 'offensive and deplorable' because it dehumanised Africans (See Chapter 15).

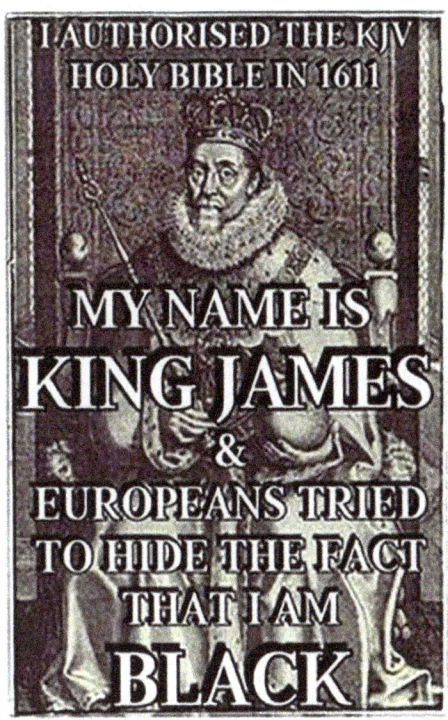

THIS image alluding to the King James V Bible — which James I commissioned one year before *The Masque of Blackness* — was posted on Twitter in 2020 as part of a disinformation campaign about British monarchs and other famous people who, despite all the evidence to the contrary, were supposedly black.

In *The Negro Rulers of Scotland and the British Isles* (2020), Dr John L Johnson wrote: 'The Bible mentions a giant Canaanite race who were of the lineage of Ham, the father of Africa. These people, who migrated from Canaan-Land to settle in Carthage Northern Africa, became great sailors and colonised Spain, Ireland, Wales, Scotland… When the dark-skinned Julius Caesar invaded Britain he fought these Blacks.' Meanwhile, Scotland was supposedly being ruled by black kings.

KING DUB of Scotland (born c928), nicknamed 'the Black', was possibly dark-skinned but (as shown right) he definitely was not a Negro. His epithet probably derived from his hair colour, and the same applies to his son, Kenneth III, who was nicknamed 'the Brown'.

On fabpedigree.com Prince Harry descends from Kenneth III's granddaughter Gruoch — the real Lady Macbeth, whose hair and skin colour are unknown — and her first husband, who was killed by her legendary second husband. Macbeth was nicknamed 'the Red King', apparently because of his red hair and ruddy complexion.

Note: The real Macbeth killed King Duncan in battle and then ruled wisely from 1040 to 1057. Forest Whitaker's depiction of the truly evil Idi Amin in *The Last King of Scotland* (2006) was influenced by Shakespeare's Macbeth, and the play also inspired a 1981 African version titled *Zeneral Makbef*.

King Dub 'the Black'

INCREDIBLY, four film versions of the famously cursed 'Scottish play' — first performed a year or so after *The Masque of Blackness* — were released in the same year (2018) that Harry married Meghan, including one in which Lady Macbeth was played by actress Akiya Henry, who has described herself as 'a black woman with a history and story to tell'. Two years later, Lady Colin Campbell told *The Sun:* 'Meghan's influence is very reminiscent of Lady Macbeth. To gain a toehold over Harry she appears to have played to his weaknesses… He is hyper-emotional, over-the-top, rushes where wise people don't and is extremely self-important.' The fact that Harry, like the real Macbeth, is red-haired makes the comparison even more noteworthy.

Prince Harry has a disputed bloodline from Lady Macbeth's unfortunate son Lulach the Fool through one of Charles II's many bastards, Charles Lennox. The king was nicknamed 'Black Boy' because of his dark skin, most likely inherited from his mother's Medici ancestors, and Lennox reportedly had a 'black complexion'.

Louise de Kerouaille and Lady Elizabeth Keppel

ACCORDING to the National Portrait Gallery's webpage, the juxtapositioning of Charles Lennox's mother Louise de Kerouaille and a young African girl in a 1682 portrait by Pierre Mignard emphasised the wealth and social standing of the duchess, and also her whiteness. Joshua Reynolds painted a similar portrait of Lennox's granddaughter Lady Elizabeth Keppel (Harry's sixth great-grandmother) in 1761, soon after Elizabeth served as one of Queen Charlotte's bridesmaids.

Charles Lennox (pictured left with an African boy) was a direct ancestor of Charles Gordon-Lennox, the nonconformist tenth Duke of Richmond, who caused a 'society scandal' in the 1960s by adopting two mixed-race girls (Maria and Naomi) who had African fathers.

(Contrary to Wikipedia, Charles Lennox did not have an illegitimate daughter named Renee who had an illegitimate daughter with the namesake son of Charles II's bastard son Charles Beauclerk, the first Duke of St Albans.)

MUCH has been written about this portrait of Queen Charlotte because Allan Ramsay allegedly made her look like a 'mulatto'. One theory is that Ramsay deliberately altered the queen's appearance so that her image could be circulated around the empire to boost the anti-slavery movement.

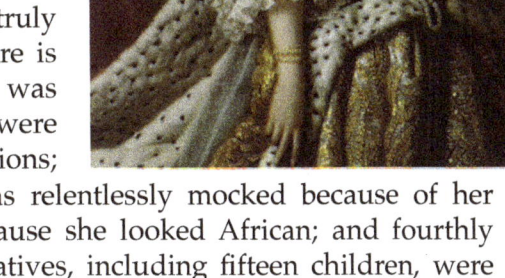

The claim that Charlotte inherited her blackness from Madragana, the Moorish mistress of the Portuguese king Afonso III (died 1279), has been well and truly debunked: firstly because there is no evidence that Madragana was black; secondly because there were so many intervening generations; thirdly because Charlotte was relentlessly mocked because of her German appearance, not because she looked African; and fourthly because all of her closest relatives, including fifteen children, were undeniably white.

Debate about Queen Charlotte's African heritage intensified in 1989 after a statue of her was unveiled in Charlotte, North Carolina. A local Methodist minister complained that the queen's 'African features' had been replaced by 'European or Caucasian appearance'. (Coincidentally, one of Meghan Markle's first known slave ancestors, Richard Ragland, was reportedly born in Chatham County, North Carolina in 1792.)

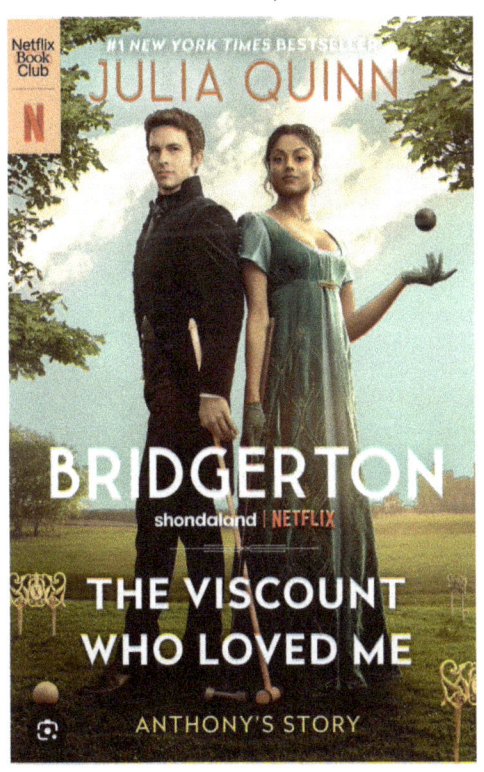

QUEEN CHARLOTTE'S alleged blackness inspired the *Bridgerton* TV series, and a prequel about her early life, which left critics deeply divided. Comments have ranged from 'a satisfying inversion of tropes' to 'preposterous and cliche-ridden' and 'soulless and vapid'. Most importantly, slavery has barely been mentioned. Harry and Meghan supposedly inspired the romance between Anthony Bridgerton, played by Jonathan Bailey, and Kate Sharma, played by Simone Ashley who has Indian Tamil heritage.

MEGHAN MARKLE has faced many racist comments about her complexion, including bizarre claims in 2022 - one year after the infamous Oprah interview — that she used 'blackface' to darken her skin at the One Young World summit. As someone commented on Reddit, 'blackface doesn't apply when you are biracial and you want to appear sun-kissed for an event'.

Shamira Ibrahim wrote on allure.com: 'Meghan Markle, though she is a biracial woman, is arguably white-passing. But even her proximity to whiteness couldn't shield her or her son from the British royal family's alleged concerns about his blackness.' (The concerned royals were later identified as Charles III and the Princess of Wales.) For Shamira, the ultimate irony was that a 'global conversation on colourism was now being centred around a woman who, within the Black community, would normally sit at the opposite end of the table.'

As 'half-royals' living in California, Prince Archie and Princess Lilibet face many years of unwelcome comments about their hair colours and complexions. In January 2023, Harry told late night TV host Stephen Colbert that both of his children had inherited his red hair. 'The Spencer gene is very, very strong,' Harry said. 'I genuinely thought at the beginning of my relationship that, should this go the distance and we have kids, that there's no way the ginger gene will stand up to my wife's genes, but I was wrong!'

While Archie Harrison Sussex will always be in his father's shadow, poor Lilibet Diana will be endlessly compared to her mother and the two women after whom she was named — her glamorous grandmother, Princess Diana, and the original Lilibet, Elizabeth II.

8 The Curse of Ham

Prince Harry's Curse

ARGUABLY the most evil and most consequential curse in world history, the so-called Curse of Ham hugely impacted many African-American ancestors of Prince Harry's children. There is also no doubt that lingering racism from this curse is still upsetting people today, including a man named Ham who has built a huge replica of Noah's Ark in America.

The best-known translation of Noah's curse is in the King James Version of the Bible which was first published in 1611, eight years before the first African slaves were sold in what is now the USA from a ship sponsored by one of Harry's ancestors (whose mother, Lady Penelope Rich, appeared in *The Masque of Blackness* before James I in 1605).

For starters, here is the King James Version's account of Noah getting drunk in Genesis 9: 'And Ham, the father of Canaan, saw the nakedness of his father, and told his two brethren without. And Shem and Japheth took a garment, and laid it upon both their shoulders, and went backward, and covered the nakedness of their father… And Noah awoke from his wine, and knew what his younger son had done unto him. And he said, Cursed be Canaan; a servant of servants shall he be unto his brethren'.

Note that the curse was not placed on Ham, but on his son Canaan, and that exactly what Ham did unto Noah is unclear (suggestions have ranged from castration and sodomy, to Ham having sex with his mother). Most importantly, there is no mention of black skin. It is also worth noting that in the hardcover copy of the New English Translation — bashed against Prince Harry's head by one of his Eton teachers — this passage ended thus: 'Cursed be Canaan! The lowest of *slaves* he will be to his brothers.'

Prince Henry the Navigator

THE FIRST interpretations of Noah's curse associating black skin with slavery were published in Portugal in the 1400s while Prince Henry the Navigator — the second spare son of King John I — was sending ships down the African coast, opening up the continent for the trans-Atlantic slave trade. (Between 1500 and the 1870s, Portuguese vessels transported about 5.8 million Africans across the Atlantic, compared to Britain's total of about 3.8 million. The Dutch king, Willem-Alexander, formally apologised in 2023 but Charles III has resisted doing the same.)

Prince Harry does not descend directly from his Portuguese namesake but he does have a bastard bloodline from the Navigator's English uncle, Henry IV. Harry also descends from Robert Rich, the second Earl of Warwick, sponsor of the Dutch-registered *White Lion* which captured about twenty Africans from a Portuguese slave ship in 1619 and transported them to the English colony of Virginia. They were not the first slaves to set foot in North America but it was 'an ignominious milestone'.

Nicholas Martiau and Harry Washington

ANOTHER of Prince Henry's ancestors, a French Huguenot named Nicholas Martiau, arrived in Jamestown, Virginia, in 1620. Martiau ended up owning several African slaves and his great-great-great-grandson, President George Washington, owned several hundred (including Harry Washington, whose incredible story has been told by Thierry Paulais). Martiau's daughter Elizabeth married a slave owner named Colonel George Reade, an Acting Governor of the colony, and their daughter Mildred married yet another slave owner named Augustine Warner Junior.

Augustine Warner Jr and his plantation

Warner's granddaughter, Mildred Warner Smith, married a son of tobacco plantation owner Edward Porteous who featured in *The Guardian* shortly before the 2023 coronation of his direct descendant Charles III. According to David Conn and Rachel Hall, Porteous was involved in buying at least 200 enslaved people from the Royal African

Company (governed by James II) in 1686. The article was based on documents discovered by Desiree Baptiste while researching her play about one of Porteous' female slaves named Cumbo. It was, said Desiree, 'a way to honour the many millions of the enslaved of the British Empire whose strangled voices remain unheard'.

There is no evidence that any of Prince Harry's American ancestors used the Curse of Ham to justify their ownership of slaves, but many racist interpretations were cited by pro-slavery campaigners in the 1700s and especially before the Civil War which started in 1861. In more recent times, the Curse of Ham was used to justify apartheid in South Africa, a subject which may have arisen when Prince Harry met Desmond Tutu two years before his death in 2021.

Source: New York Public Library

UP TO ten million Africans were enslaved in the USA between 1619 and 1861, and many were ripped from their families at slave auctions. Marriages between slaves were illegal, so all of their children were considered illegitimate. As well, under the notorious 'one drop' rule', anyone with an African ancestor was considered black, regardless of their skin colour.

The total number of Meghan Markle's slave ancestors is unknown but we do know that they had surnames —including Betts, Ragland, Ritchie and Russell — which were probably forced on them by their owners. According to wikitree.com Harry's children may descend from an African man named Bena — born near the Ivory Coast around 1770, and possibly of the Fanti tribe — who died in Henty County, Georgia. Bena was given the surname Ragland which first appeared in Virginia in the 1600s.

It is not uncommon for white descendants of slave owners to have some African DNA for the same reason that many black descendants have some European DNA. The odds of Prince Harry and Meghan Markle having a common ancestor who once lived in Virginia are vanishingly small. But, once again, detailed analysis of DNA samples from both Prince Harry and Meghan Markle could be very revealing.

Meghan Markle Is Proof That Black Negro People Were Cursed By Noah

Posted on January 16, 2020 by Mary-Tamar was Jean

READERS can decide for themselves if the writer of this blog, who describes herself as a 'black woman with kinky hair', has a fair and reasonable opinion: 'The outrage and outcry of Meghan's so called racism proves the self hatred of black people. It proves that they are not a normal race, they loathe themselves and would rather be white, actually would rather be mixed race because they will get to enjoy being called black whilst living in white privilege… I always knew that black people were cursed by Noah, but Lord, I never knew that the curse would be permanent like this.'

Ken Ham and his ark

The final words on this subject are from Ken Ham, the Australian 'young Earth creationist' who has built a replica of Noah's Ark — with plenty of dinosaurs — in Williamstown, Kentucky. In a blog at answersingenesis.org titled Was Ham Cursed?, Ken writes: 'I often jokingly say that I'm pretty sensitive about this issue, since my last name is Ham. Seriously, I think it's important that people understand that we don't teach that dark-skinned peoples are "cursed"… In fact, Charles Darwin himself had some very racist views, which he expressed in *The Descent of Man*… [So] let's stop talking about the supposed curse of Ham. There was NO curse of Ham!'

9

Prince Harry's Curse

Harry's slave ancestor?

PREPOSTEROUS as it may sound, both Prince Harry and Meghan Markle possibly descend from an African woman raped by one of his slave-owning ancestors in a sugar plantation in Barbados in the 1660s. It is also remotely possible that that woman was branded with the initials of James II, whose daughter Henrietta FitzJames is one of many royal bastards in Harry's pedigree.

In his 2006 book about slavery and capitalism, Dr Simon David Smith wrote: 'In the case of Barbados, a tradition exists that a female member of the Lascelles family was coloured.' By 1937, the sixth Earl of Harewood, Henry Lascelles, was corresponding with E M Shilstone, the archivist and librarian of the Barbados Museum, on the subject of Frances Ball's paternity. One of the issues that perplexed the earl and Shilstone was the absence of Frances' name from her father's will.

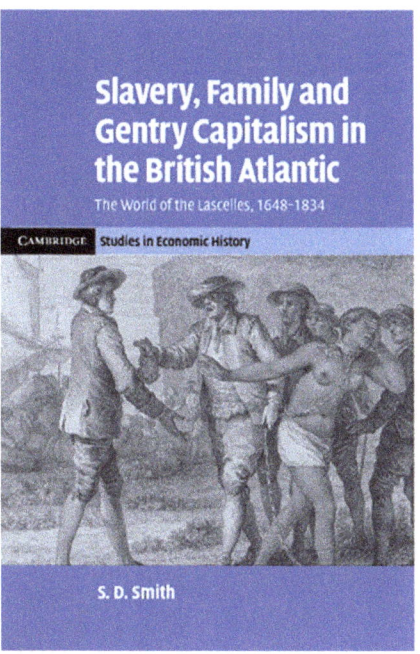

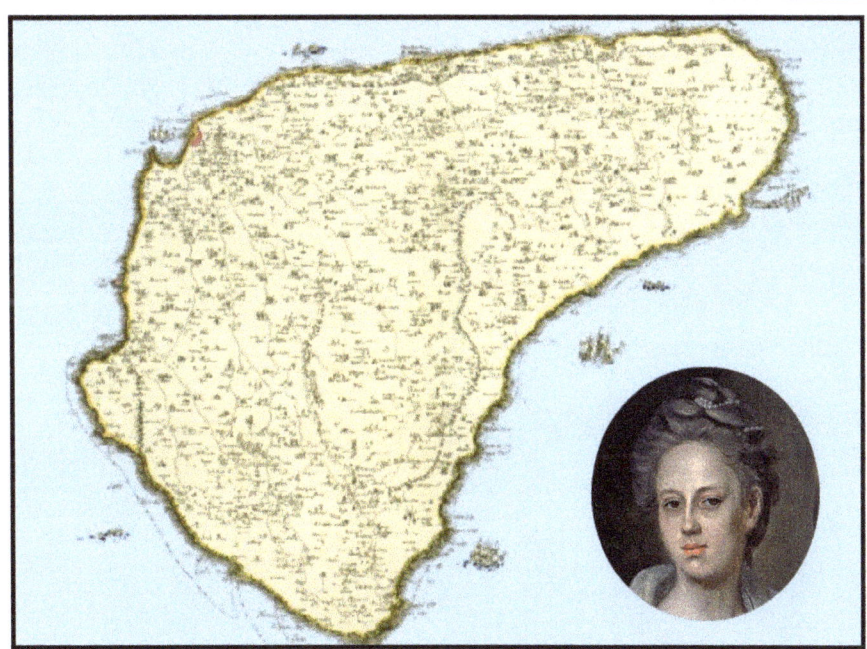

Frances Ball Photo: Wikitree

IN 1953, Shilstone received an enquiry from John Hill of Berkshire regarding a 'black woman' in the Lascelles pedigree. Hill speculated that Frances Ball 'was a throw back who surprised and shocked her father by showing her dusty parentage'. Shilstone was particularly interested in Frances' mother Catherine Dubois, also known as Katherine Hole, whose mother — according to Cookie Crumbs Ancestry (gdcooke.org) — was Katharine Gillhampton, born around 1665. Princess Diana descended from Frances Ball's son Edward Lascelles, the first Earl of Harewood, through James Hamilton, the first Duke of Abercorn.

Edward Lascelles and Harewood House

JOHN HILL wrote to E M Shilstone again in 1960, presenting new information obtained from a Lascelles descendant named Ian Rankin. Rankin had told Hill that, in his family, the mysterious black woman was called 'the mistake in the sugar plantation'. (It should also be noted that plantation owners routinely bred their own slaves to lessen their dependence on trans-Atlantic slave traders.)

While there is no suggestion of mixed race in a surviving portrait of Frances Ball held at Harewood House, Dr Simon Smith concluded that 'the notion of her partial African ancestry was never erased from the Lascelles' family history and it is still significant that branches of the family *remembered* her as being a black woman'.

(Also hanging in Harewood House — built in the 1760s with profits from slavery — is a portrait of well-known black actor David Harewood whose ancestors worked on one of the Lascelles' plantations. David has supported the current earl's efforts to expose the horrors of slavery, and is also campaigning for a government apology for Britain's involvement in the slave trade.)

Elizabeth II in Barbados, 1966

The question of Frances Ball's colour was 'an extremely sensitive matter' for the Lascelles family because the sixth Earl of Harewood — depicted in the 2019 film *Downton Abbey* by Andrew Havill, who also appeared in *The King's Speech* — married George VI's sister Princess Mary. That explains why Elizabeth II stayed at the Lascelles' sugar plantation during her visit to Barbados in 1966.

Prince Harry in Barbados, 2016

SHORTLY before Harry visited Barbados in 2016, Nalini Mohabir and Jermain Ostiana posed a very pertinent question in *The Guardian*: 'Why, in these post-colonial times, is a member of the British monarchy, an embodiment of anglo-imperialism, invited to mark independence.' Nalini and Jermain invited Harry to 'co-conspire in our decolonising vision and engage in an act of royal rebellion by thinking about what liberation might mean for his girlfriend's family, and others who walk in slavery's shadow. Prince Harry, show us how woke you are, and atone for the royals' institutional role in slavery.'

To his credit, Harry addressed the issue of slavery in his memoir *Spare* (2023): 'Does the Crown… rest upon lands obtained and secured when the system was unjust and wealth was generated by exploited workers and thuggery, annexation and enslaved people? Can anyone deny it?'

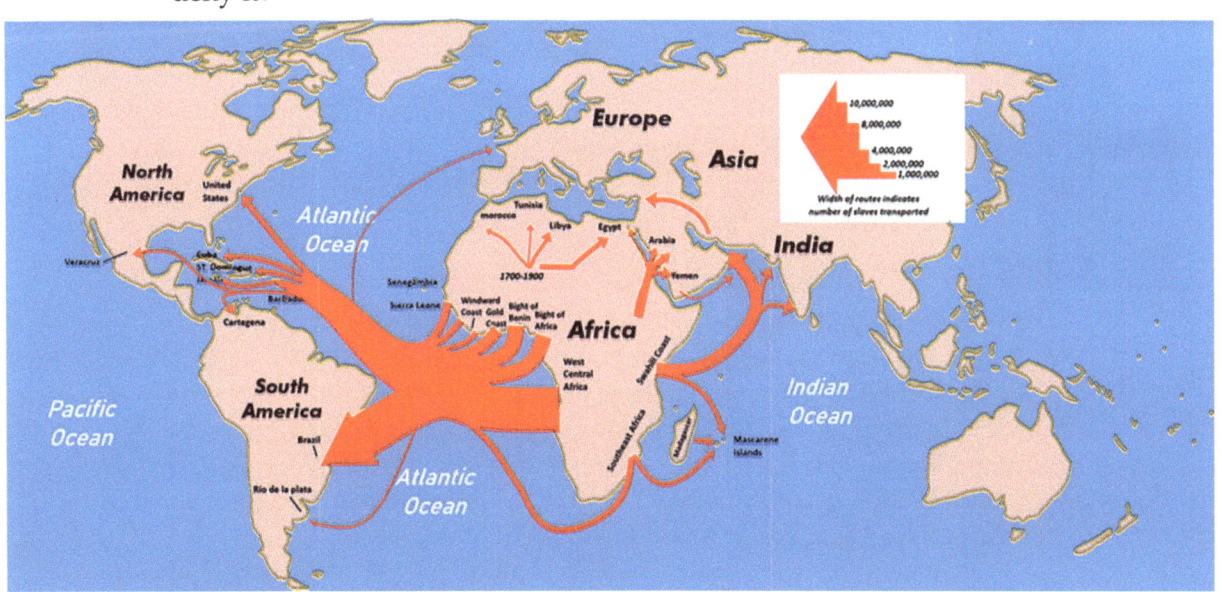

FROM 1660 to the Glorious Revolution of 1688, the Royal African Company shipped around 100,000 slaves from Western Africa to the Caribbean with a significant number dying at sea. Katharine Gillhampton's mother, known only as Elizabeth, may have been one of those slaves, many of whom were branded with the initials of James II (DY for Duke of York), or the initials of the company (RAC). The irons were dipped in palm oil so that flesh would not adhere to the metal.

THIS Romanesque statue of James II in Trafalgar Square, and a conventional statue of his older brother Charles II in Soho Square, attracted a lot of attention during Black Lives Matter protests in 2020. An artist named Rachel Reid adorned both statues with branding irons topped with the elephant and castle symbol of the Royal African Company. 'My own artistic intervention is a modest contribution to our discussion about how slavery is woven into English history, and therefore to the racism of today,' Rachel wrote. The Trafalgar Square iron was removed within hours, but the one in Soho Square remained for two weeks.

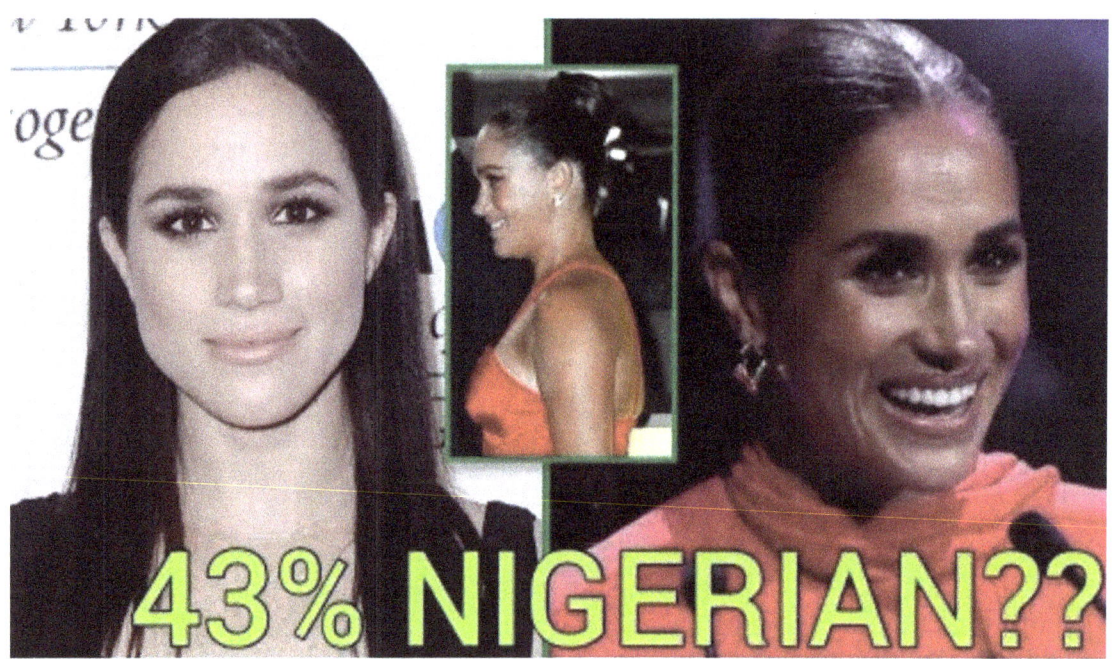

THE Duchess of Sussex has reportedly claimed that she is 43 per cent Nigerian and 69 per cent Jamaican. The first claim is plausible but the second is nonsense because Meghan's father, from whom she gets 50 per cent of her DNA, has German, Dutch and British ancestors. (Coincidentally, Harry's Dutch-English ancestor Henry Bentinck, the first Duke of Portland, owned 287 slaves while he was governor of Jamaica from 1721 until his death in 1726.)

Researchers have found a higher than expected percentage of Nigerian ancestry in slave descendants across the United States, which suggests that many of their ancestors were shipped from the Caribbean. In fact, about 500,000 African slaves who landed in North America came via islands, including Barbados and Jamaica, compared to only 388,000 slaves who were transported directly from numerous modern-day countries, including Senegal, Gambia, Sierra Leone, Ghana, Benin, Cameroon and Gabon.

IT IS NOT impossible that nearly all of Meghan's maternal slave ancestors came from what is now Nigeria, and that begs a question: Do Harry and Meghan have a Nigerian ancestor in common who may have lived during the 1660s? Needless to say, detailed analysis of Harry's and Meghan's DNA would be very informative.

Another intriguing possibility is that Harry's children have inherited haplogroup L through an all-female bloodline from Nigeria's Igbo tribe which reputedly descends from one of the lost tribes of Israel (See Chapter 12).

Prince Harry has a special relationship with Prince Seeiso of Lesotho (which, as shown above, is surrounded by South Africa). The two royal spares became 'like brothers' around 2003 when both were mourning the deaths of their mothers. Three years later they founded the Sentebale charity which helps young people cope with HIV.

Lesotho inspired Wakanda, home of the superhero Black Panther who first appeared in a comic book in 1966 (coincidentally, the year that Prince Seeiso was born).

While Harry is also friendly with Nelson Mandela's granddaughter Ndileka, she reportedly called out the Sussexes in 2023 for using Mandela's legacy to promote their Netflix series *Live to Lead*. 'I admire Harry for having the confidence to break away from an institution as iconic as the royal family,' Ndileka told *The Australian*. "Grandad rebelled against an arranged marriage to find his own path in life, but it comes at a price [because] you have to then fund your own life. I've made peace with people using grandad's name, but it's still deeply upsetting.' Ndileka later claimed she was misquoted.

10

Theodore and Eliza

Prince Harry's Curse

PRINCE HARRY is genetically linked to British imperialism — especially in relation to tea, sugar and opium — through his extremely rare mitochondrial DNA inherited from Eliza Kewark, the Indian-Armenian wife of Theodore Forbes who worked for the accursed East India Company in the early 1800s.

Like many spare sons from the Scottish gentry, Theodore sought his fortune in India at a time when opium was being traded for Chinese tea, and also when 'East India sugar' was being promoted as an alternative to Caribbean sugar dependent on slavery. Repercussions from these 'evils of empire' are still being felt today.

The Portuguese princess Catherine of Braganza, wife of Prince Harry's ancestor Charles II, did not introduce tea drinking to Britain in 1662, but she greatly boosted demand for 'the cup that cheers but not inebriates'. It is also significant that, as part of Catherine's dowry, Britain acquired the port of Bombay (where Theodore Forbes worked for the East India Company).

As Billie Cohen wrote in a BBC article titled 'The true story behind England's tea obsession' (2017), prior to Catherine's arrival, 'tea was being consumed there only as a medicine, supposedly invigorating the body and keeping the spleen free of obstructions'. But because the young queen used the 'pick-me-up' as part of her daily routine, it soon became popular among the nobility. Eventually, the habit percolated down to the lower classes, who also consumed a lot of coffee and hot chocolate which, like tea, was sweetened with sugar.

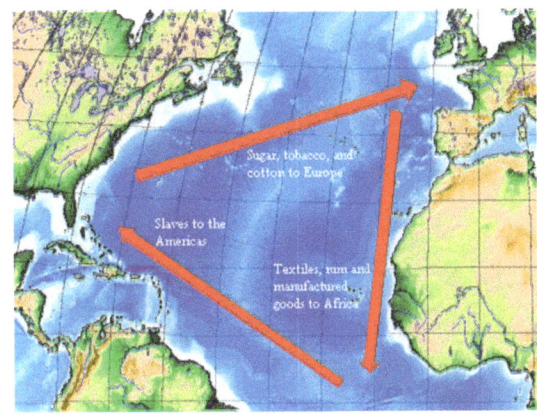 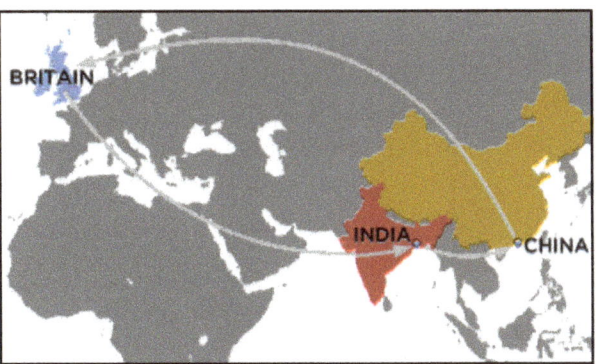

The Opium Triangle

THESE TWO maps show the triangular shipping routes which enabled African slaves to be traded for Caribbean sugar, and for Indian opium to be traded for Chinese tea. The latter trade devastated the economies of two nations, which now have a combined population of around 2.8 billion people, and it is long overdue for the British government to apologise.

In 2014, shortly before Elizabeth II met the Chinese Premier, Hong Kong University professor Jean-Pierre Lehmann wrote in the *Financial Times:* 'A sincere apology would serve to remind us Europeans that while we admonish the Chinese today to be "responsible stakeholders", when we were on top we did not play by the rules, because there were no rules, except for the rule of sheer brute force.'

THANKS to Harry's ancestor Charles Grey (right), the British Prime Minister best-known for a certain tea blend, another of Harry's ancestors — East India Company director George Smith of Croydon (who probably knew a lot about opium) — was richly compensated in the 1830s for 461 Jamaican slaves. Altogether, thousands of British slave owners received billions of pounds in today's money — through a loan not paid off until 2015 — but, shockingly, slaves throughout the empire got absolutely nothing.

Harry is familiar with Twinings tea (which has a royal warrant) and also with opium, possibly from personal usage, but mainly because a large percentage of the world's illegal supply came from Afghanistan's Helmand province where he served in the early 2000s (See next chapter).

IN THE *Pirates of the Caribbean* backstory, Jack Sparrow — like Harry's ancestor Theodore Forbes — joins the East India Company as a young man. Sparrow leaves the company after refusing to transport African slaves; is later branded with the letter P; and is temporarily cursed after taking an Aztec coin. Theodore Forbes was much less adventurous, but he did deal with pirates while working as an East India Company coffee buyer in Mocha, a port at the entrance to the Red Sea.

Prince Harry has been dubbed Captain Harry Sparrow on a short YouTube video and, coincidentally, one of his Californian neighbours is *Pirates of the Caribbean* star Orlando Bloom.

The 1770 Bengal famine

THE EAST INDIA COMPANY was truly evil, as evidenced by the 1770 famine in Bengal which Kendra Bell detailed in an online article titled 'Genocide or Disaster' (2021). She concluded: 'Even though the East India Company and the British imperial state were well-informed about the threat of famine in Bengal, authorities took no measures to protect the population. Rather, the company acted to increase economic opportunities… privileging corporate profit over human life, which resulted in the deaths of ten million people.'

A few years later, Edmund Burke feared that 'this cursed company would, at last, like a viper, be the destruction of the country which fostered it at its bosom'. Alas, the company was too big to fail and was bailed out by the British government.

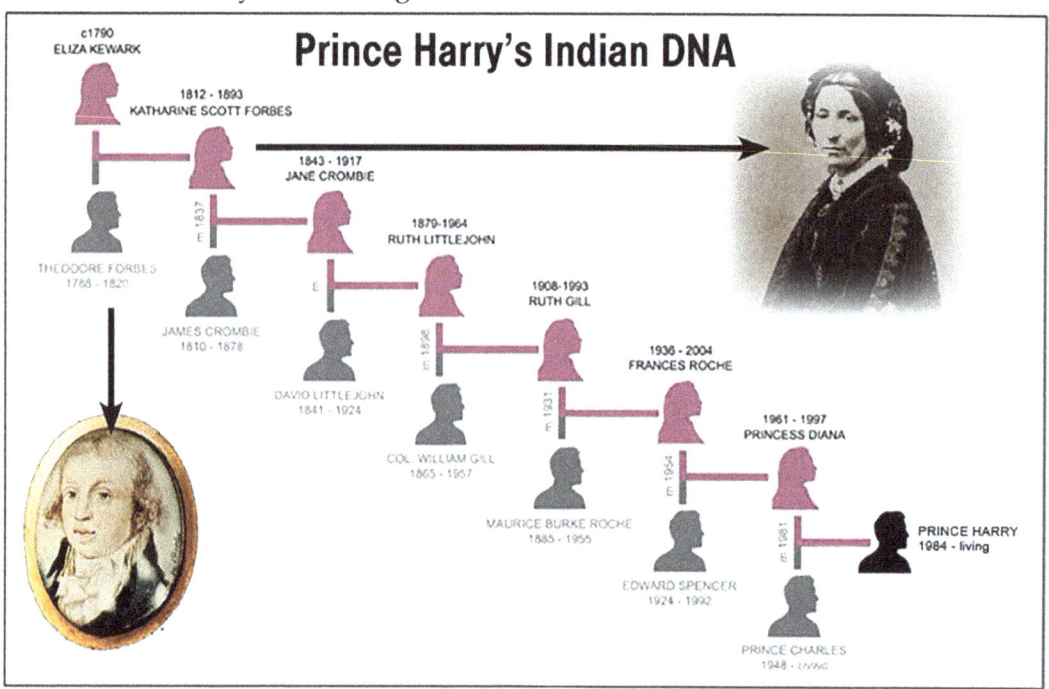

Neither Prince Harry or his brother have disputed the claim — first made in 2013, based on DNA samples from several maternal relatives — that they have extremely rare Indian R30b mitochondrial DNA inherited from Eliza Kewark's daughter Katherine Scott Forbes. None of that DNA has been inherited by Harry's children because they carry Meghan's mtDNA, possibly one of the L haplogroups inherited from an African ancestor. Note also that Harry's Y-DNA is R1b which is common in Britain.

THE FIRST media reports about Eliza Kewark described her as a 'dark-skinned native of Bombay' who had an illegitimate daughter with Theodore Forbes. Susan Harvard dispelled those rumours in her 2018 book based on family papers in the library of Aberdeen University. Eliza's poignant letters to her absent husband, dictated to a Parsi scribe in broken English, were signed in Armenian script: 'Your affectionate Mrs Forbes'. In short, like Meghan Markle, Eliza was a biracial victim of racism.

Eliza's death date in India is unknown but Theodore died in 1820 on a ship returning to Britain. Katherine Scott Forbes — whose nanny Fazagool may have been an African slave — died in Aberdeen, Scotland in 1893 aged 81.

HARRY'S ancestor Queen Charlotte, now widely known because of the *Bridgerton* TV series, led a boycott against Caribbean sugar produced by slaves. In James Gillray's 1792 satirical print (above) the queen urges her daughters to taste unsweetened tea: 'O my dear Creatures, do but Taste it! You can't think how nice it is without Sugar: and then consider how much Work you'll save the poor Blackeemoors.' (In 2017, Princess Michael of Kent was accused of racism after she wore a blackamoor brooch to an event attended by Meghan Markle.)

ANTI-SLAVERY campaigners promoted East India sugar as an ethical alternative to the slave-grown product, but the truth was somewhat different. In an online article dated 2015, Andrea Major wrote: 'The exploitative and often oppressive nature of colonial governance in India under the British East India Company is rarely discussed in the context of East Indian sugar. This is a notable omission, since agricultural production in India during this period (and also more recently) was directly linked to extreme poverty… as well as the local use of domestic and agricultural slavery.'

In 2019, while pregnant, Meghan Markle reportedly got Prince Harry to give up tea (as well as coffee and alcohol). According to Lauren Evans at jezebel.com Harry's new lifestyle made him calmer and healthier, but also 'super boring' and 'no longer English'.

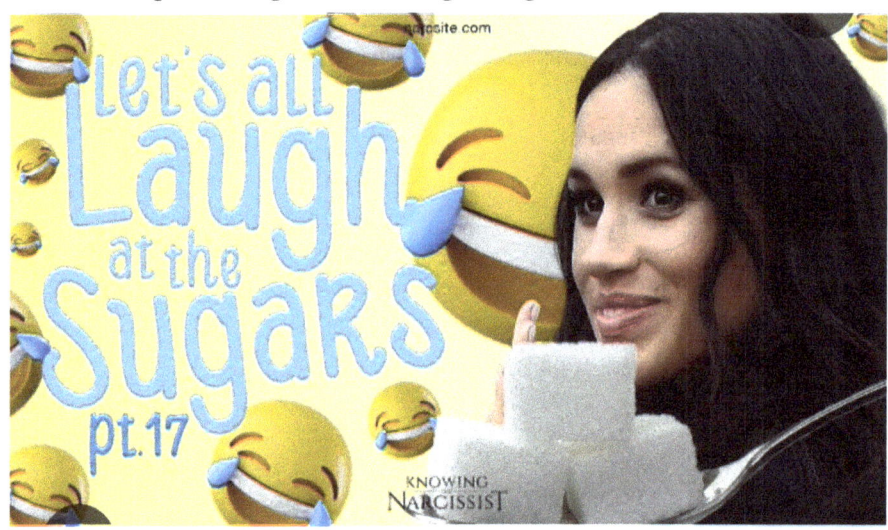

At the same time that Harry was forgoing tea and coffee, Meghan's 'superfans' were being ridiculed on social media with a bizarre nickname. While no one knows the origin or exact meaning of the term 'Sugars', it is undeniably racist and nasty. 'Don't be fooled by the sweet name, wrote one Twitter user. 'They are extremely aggressive and have even threatened Kate [Middleton].'

One sensational claim about Meghan, allegedly supported by actor Liam Neeson, is that 'sugar daddies' showered her with money and expensive gifts before she met Prince Harry. It has also been claimed, with absolutely no proof, that Meghan had a secret baby with one of these men.

On a happier note, fans of the 2003 Christmas film *Love Actually* fondly remember Neeson as the stepfather of redheaded Sam whose romance with an American biracial girl named Joanna — while dealing with the death of his mother— supposedly predicted Harry and Meghan.

11

Prince Harry's Curse

The Graveyard of Empires

THE NOTION that Prince Harry is afflicted by a multi-layered curse with biblical connotations is exemplified by Afghanistan where he is regarded as a modern-day crusader. This so-called 'Graveyard of Empires' has a border known as 'Durand's Curse' and is a claimant to the Kohinoor diamond, which has cursed the royal family since 1850. The country also inspired a Rudyard Kipling poem which includes the line: 'Curse, curse, curse of a soldier'.

To start with, Harry — like his uncle Prince Andrew in the Falklands War — was allowed to risk his life in Afghanistan only because, in Harry's words, 'the spare could always be spared'. This also explains why the second sons of Harry's ancestors Henry II, King John and Henry III went on crusades to the Holy Land while the oldest sons remained close to home.

Not surprisingly, Harry received a lot of flak after revealing a 'kill count' of 25 while serving with NATO forces in Helmand Province. In his memoir *Spare* (2023), Harry wrote: 'It wasn't a number that gave me any satisfaction. But neither was it a number that made me feel ashamed. Naturally I'd have preferred not to have that number on my military CV, on my mind, but by the same token I'd have preferred to live in a world in which there was no Taliban, a world without war.'

Harry referred to a process known as 'othering'. 'You can't kill people if you think of them as people,' he wrote. 'They were chess pieces removed from the board.'

HARRY'S comments were condemned by the highly respected Colonel Tim Collins: 'That's not how you behave in the army; it's not how we think,' Collins said. 'We don't do notches on the rifle butt.' Another army veteran told *The Guardian:* 'I've never heard anyone talk about kill counts, it's crass and frankly cringeworthy. Taking a life is the most serious thing you can ever do on ops, serious people don't talk it up as a game to shift a few books.'

James Jeffrey had a much different take in *The Spectator* (January 2023). 'It is refreshing to hear someone talking about what it was like in Afghanistan and being listened to for once,' he wrote. 'The generals responsible for the operation have been promoted or retired with fantastic pensions while the soldiers and young officers who served there — like Harry — have been left to shoulder the burden of the Afghanistan curse. For too many that weight has been too much and they have taken their lives.'

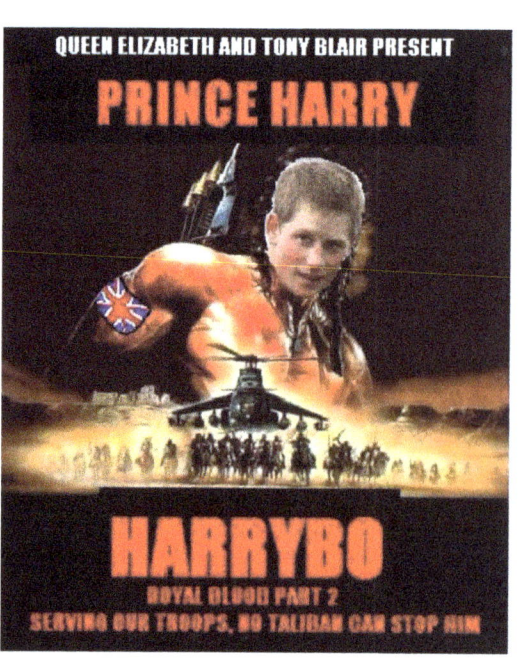

The so-called War on Terror was an abysmal failure in Afghanistan; it should also be noted that the Taliban's ban on opium production has been hugely successful. As for Afghanistan being the 'Graveyard of Empires' — most notably Britain's and Russia's — Sylvester Stallone said it best in *Rambo III* after hearing Alexander The Great's famous quote about 'the venom of the cobra and teeth of the tiger': 'You guys don't take any shit.'

WHILE Afghanistan is, presumably, not suffering from a curse laid by the legendary Queen Gandhari, it is suffering because of the Durand Line drawn through the Pashtun homeland by a servant of the British Raj. In his acclaimed 2017 book, *Durand's Curse,* Rajiv Dogra wrote: 'The terrorism that torments the world today can, in an important way, be traced back to the British grab of 40,000-square miles of the Afghan territory in 1893.'

The astonishing claim that the Pashtun people, like the British and Americans, descend from Israel's legendary lost tribes — which were all cursed in different ways — was demolished by Zaman Stanizai on cambridge.org in December 2023: 'Its biblical claims are anecdotal, its historical documentation is inconsistent, its geographic claims are incoherent, and its linguistic assertions are implausible.' However, despite all that, the claim had 'hit a raw nerve' in both Afghanistan and Pakistan.

The last stand at Gandamak

Fifty years before Mortimer Durand drew his infamous line, remnants of a British invasion force — which included soldiers from the East India Company — made one of Britain's most famous last stands. William Barnes Wollen's painting (above) brings to mind the last verse of Rudyard Kipling's poem, The Young British Soldier: 'When you're wounded and left on Afghanistan's plains, and the women come out to cut up what remains, jest roll to your rifle and blow out your brains, and go to your gawd like a soldier.'

Hypothetically, if Meghan has an affair with one of Harry's mates, he should follow some other advice in Kipling's poem: 'Make 'im take 'er and keep 'er: that's Hell for them both, An' you're shut o' the curse of a soldier. Curse, curse, curse of a soldier.'

AS SHOWN above, Kipling's personal symbol was an ancient and uncontroversial flipped version of the Nazi swastika worn by Prince Harry to a party in 2005. Six years later, soon after the assassination of Osama Bin Laden, the UK-based group Muslims Against Crusades released a hate video titled 'Harry the Nazi'. One of the comments echoed those made against Harry's crusader ancestors: 'May Allah curse and destroy him.'

George Orwell called the Indian-born Kipling, the author of much-loved classics such as *The Jungle Book* and *Kim,* a 'jingo-imperialist' and described his work as 'morally insensitive and aesthetically disgusting'. However, Orwell conceded that the 'gutter patriot' had said bitter things about Britain and imperialism. In short, Kipling has a very mixed legacy.

Kipling's most popular poem 'If' — which includes a line about walking with kings and not losing the common touch — is often compared to another poem that is well-known to Prince Harry, William Ernest Henley's 'Invictus', which ends: 'I am the master of my fate, I am the captain of my soul'. (Obviously, Harry's mastery of his fate is debatable.)

In his 2023 Netflix documentary titled *Heart of Invictus,* Harry spoke about his personal trauma after leaving Afghanistan in 2012. 'Somewhere after that there was an unravelling,' he said. 'But the stuff that was coming up was from 1997, from the age of 12, losing my mum at such a young age'. Diana was supposedly afflicted by 'The Spencer Curse' (See Page 73).

MEANWHILE, the royal family is still being cursed by the Kohinoor diamond which was gifted to Queen Victoria by the East India Company in 1850. According to legend, men who obtain it will 'own the world, but will also know all its misfortunes. Only God or woman can wear it with impunity'.

Harry reflected on the accursed gem in his great-grandmother's crown at her funeral in 2002: 'At the centre of the cross was a diamond the size of a cricket ball…the Great Diamond of the World, a 105-karat monster called the Koh-i-Noor… "Acquired" by the British Empire at its zenith. Stolen, some thought.'

Given that four countries claim the Kohinoor — Afghanistan, Pakistan, India and Iran — it is likely to remain in Britain for quite some time with its curse being blamed for everything bad that has happened to the royal family, from COVID-19 to Charles III's cancer, and maybe 'Megxit' as well.

Absent the Kohinoor, Charles III's coronation featured three pieces of the infamous Cullinan diamond found in South Africa in 1905. Originally more than 3100 carats, the gem was cut into nine large stones — including The Great Star of Africa — and around one hundred smaller stones, all of which symbolise the evils of imperialism. 'What we want is not just the return of the Cullinan [but] the return of our humanity,' said Professor Everisto Benvera. 'We want those who perpetrated the slave trade and colonialism to acknowledge their wrongdoing, first and foremost, and then we can talk about reparations.'

Prince Harry and Meghan once planned to live in South Africa and may end up there if pathological liar Donald Trump is re-elected and revokes Harry's visa for lying about his drug use (which he wrote about in *Spare*).

12

Prince Harry's Curse

Biblical Bloodlines

DOES Prince Harry descend from the second sons of Noah, Abraham, Isaac and King David through the offspring of Jesus and Mary Magdalene? No. But, as Dan Brown demonstrated with *The Da Vinci Code*, why let the truth get in the way of a good story, especially when British royals have believed in biblical nonsense for more than a thousand years.

'The Secret of England's Greatness' (above), which depicts Harry's great-great-great-great-grandmother Queen Victoria giving a Bible to an African ambassador, was completed in 1861, the same year that the Reverend Frederick Glover published a pamphlet — reprinted in 2024 (inset) — which supposedly proved that Victoria descended from King David.

This seemingly harmless notion, combined with the claim that Anglo Saxon people descend from the legendary lost tribes of Israel, was the basis of an antisemitic, white supremacist doctrine that helped to establish an empire, upon which the sun never set, and also encouraged American exceptionalism. Bob Dylan said it all in 'With God on Our Side'.

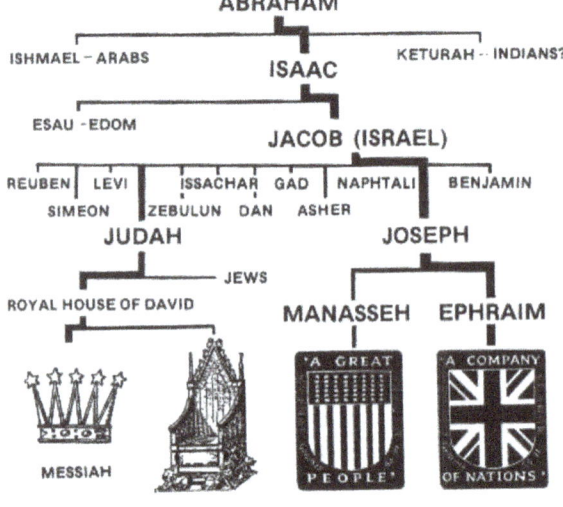

BRITISH monarchs and the Messiah supposedly belong to the Royal House of David with a bloodline through the second sons of Abraham and Isaac. According to legend, the so-called Stone of Scone in the coronation chair is Jacob's Pillow which somehow ended up in Scotland, from whence it was stolen by Prince Harry's ancestor Edward I. Note also that the Jews have a different bloodline from Jacob's British and American descendants who supposedly get all of God's blessings.

In short, the expectation of millions of deluded Christians is that Jesus will one day return and actually sit on the throne that is currently occupied by Prince Harry's adulterous father who — thanks to the monstrous, monastery-burning Henry VIII — is Supreme Governor of the Church of England and Defender of the Faith.

CHRIST'S possibly imminent return to rule the whole world from London raises some very big and small questions: Will he point out that Jacob's Pillow is a fake, and so are the alleged shards of the True Cross that the Pope gave to Charles III — as was the piece that Pope Marinus gave to Alfred the Great in 884; and another piece, in the famous Cross Gneth, which along with some of the Virgin Mary's breast milk, may still remain under St George's Chapel in which Prince Harry was married. And the biggest question of all? Will the 'not religious' Harry and his wife be invited to Christ's coronation?

Ironically, it is slightly more likely that Prince Harry descends from Abraham's first son Ishmael through the Prophet Muhammad than it is for Harry to descend from Ishmael's younger brother Isaac through Jesus. The alleged bloodline from Muhammad — who was reputedly born without a foreskin — is through Zaida of Seville, a Muslim princess who was born around 1070.

In his memoir, Harry wrote about training in a 'Christian army' to fight Muslim terrorists. After a staged kidnapping, he was tormented about his mother's relationship with Dodi al-Fayed, who both died in a car crash in Paris in 1997. 'Your mother was pregnant when she died,' said a female interrogator. 'With your sibling? A Muslim baby!' Harry silently screamed at the woman as someone else spat in his face.

Jacob and Rachel

Royal fans who are praying for Harry to reconcile with brother William can take comfort from what happened to Jacob after he clashed with older brother Esau, went into exile, and married Rachel (which is Meghan's real first name, and also the first name of her *Suits* character). The good news is that Jacob and Esau had an emotional reunion; the bad news is that Jacob unwittingly cursed Rachel after she disrespected her father by feigning menstruation, the so-called Curse of Eve, and died after giving birth to her second child.

The Holy Foreskin

THE Holy Prepuce from Jesus' circumcision (above) was allegedly obtained by Henry V to benefit his young wife Catherine of Valois (from whom Harry probably descends through Henry VIII's illegitimate daughter Catherine Carey). Some say that Henry V placed the foreskin in his wedding bed as a fertility symbol; others say it eased Queen Catherine's pain as she delivered the future Henry VI. Either way, up to twenty different foreskins of Jesus were floating around Europe during the Middle Ages so, as with the True Cross, there was a lot of fakery.

According to his memoir, Prince Harry has been snipped so he is in accordance with the covenant that God made with Abraham. But, unfortunately for Harry, and everyone else who wants redemption, he also has to circumcise his heart. Jeremiah 4:4 clearly states: 'Remove the foreskin of your hearts… lest my wrath go forth like fire, and burn with none to quench it, because of the evil of your deeds.'

Strictly speaking, Harry is an adulterer because he married Meghan while her first husband was still alive. And as depicted by the Monty Python crew in *Life of Brian*, the penalty for adultery is very unpleasant.

WHILE the odds of Prince Harry being a direct descendant of Jesus and Mary Magdalene (above) are roughly the same as Harry being elected Pope, he does descend from the Sinclair (or St Clair) family which features in *The Da Vinci Code*. William 'the Seemly' St Clair allegedly accompanied St Margaret to Scotland with a piece of the True Cross (also known as The Holy Rood); Henry Sinclair, the Earl of Orkney, allegedly discovered America before Columbus; and the earl's grandson William started building Rosslyn Chapel in 1446.

Much of what has been written about mysterious carvings in the chapel, south of Edinburgh, is probably wrong. In particular, there is no proof that William Sinclair belonged to the legendary Knights Templar, and theories about the Holy Grail are ridiculous. (Google Lady Catherine Stewart and fabpedigree.com to learn more about Harry's Sinclair connections).

DAN BROWN had a lot to answer for after his bestselling novel was published in 2003, including damage to churches by people searching for the Holy Grail, and an alleged curse on the Sony Corporation which financed the film version. Brown was also accused of plagiarism, which was ironic because the authors he stole from based their book on the Priory of Sion hoax perpetrated by a convicted French fraudster named Pierre Plantard. As one of Plantard's associates admitted: 'I don't know why people try to make such a big thing out of nothing.'

A surprising number of people firmly believe David Icke's bonkers claim that the royal family are 'shape-shifting, reptilian lizards' whose bizarre rituals were allegedly witnessed by Princess Diana. 'Look at ancient texts and the Bible,' the former footballer once said. 'Do you really think that the snake in the Garden of Eden was really a snake?' Does this mean that one of Harry's reptilian ancestors cursed mankind forever by getting Eve to eat an apple? Hopefully someone puts that question to King Jesus at his first press conference.

On a more serious note, Icke has added to Prince Harry's trauma by claiming that his mother was 'ritualistically sacrificed' by senior royals, including his father and grandparents.

13
Harry, Hamlet and Freud

Prince Harry's Curse

CURSED or not, Prince Harry will forever be linked to two tragic princes who inspired the 'father of psychoanalysis', Sigmund Freud. This is especially fitting because Harry's paternal grandfather — whose mother was brutally mistreated by Freud — was a Prince of Greece (like Oedipus) and Denmark (like Hamlet). And who can forget Harry's hilarious story about his mother's face cream and his 'frozen todger'.

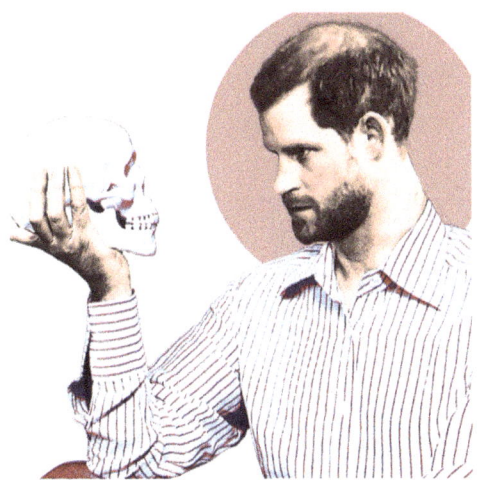

Harry wrote about Hamlet in his memoir: 'Hmmm: Lonely prince, obsessed with dead parent, watches remaining parent fall in love with dead parent's usurper …? I slammed it shut. No, thank you.' If Harry had read further he might have related to Hamlet's famous lament: 'The time is out of joint: O cursed spite, That ever I was born to set it right!'

The result of Harry's agonising —'To split or not to split' — was 'Megxit', described by Gary Nunn at abc.net.au as 'a pun waiting to be written by the British tabloid press, baying for blood since they could no longer illegally hack phones.' (Note that Megxit is misogynistic because it puts all the blame on Meghan, so Hexit is a fairer alternative.)

HISTORIAN David Starkey made two nasty claims in 2022: that Prince Harry had 'married his mother', and that Meghan had 'all Diana's bad aspects, and none of the good'. Starkey added: 'If we say that she's trying to replay Diana, I'm afraid we are reminded of Karl Marx: history first is tragedy, with Diana, and then I'm afraid it is farce with Meghan and Harry.' The Sussexes have been farcical at times, but there is nothing surprising about men marrying women with the same values as their mothers.

It also turns out the so-called Oedipus and Electra complexes have resulted in a lot of sexual abuse being ignored, starting with Freud himself.

Princess Alice and Sigmund Freud

HARRY'S great-grandmother, Princess Alice of Battenberg, was treated by Freud around 1930 after she was diagnosed with schizophrenia. Freud wrongly blamed everything on Alice's religious and sexual fantasies; and he also repeatedly X-rayed her ovaries, against her objections, in order to 'cool her down'. As Alice's character says in *The Crown* TV series, Freud 'was not a kind man'.

In stark contrast to her daughters, who married high-ranking Nazis, Princess Alice risked her life to save Jews during World War II and is renowned in Israel as 'Righteous Among the Nations'. Harry was made fully aware of this history after the 2005 uproar concerning his Nazi costume.

IN HER *New Yorker* review of *Spare* titled 'The Haunting of Prince Harry', Rebecca Mead credited his ghost writer J R Moehringer (above) for all of the literary allusions, without which *Spare* would have been vastly inferior. There are several lighthearted references to Hamlet, plus an embellished account of Harry's meeting with his father and brother in the Frogmore burial ground. Why were they there, Harry never asked, lurking in that 'undiscover'd country, from whose bourn no traveller returns?"

Mead concluded: 'The unlettered Prince has gained in life what Hamlet achieved only in death: his own story shaped on his own terms, thanks to the intervention of a skillful Horatio [Moehringer]. You might almost call it Harry's crowning achievement.'

Like many of Shakespeare's plays, *Hamlet* has been a rich source for students of psychoanalysis. According to the blurb on amazon.com James E Groves' book *Hamlet on the Couch* covers basic concepts such as the 'good-enough' mother, the compulsion to repeat, and the death instinct. Groves also deals with 'the most radical feature of psychoanalysis', self-examination. Too much of that has, almost certainly, made Harry's curse even worse.

In 2021, in the *New York Post*, Maureen Callahan accused Harry of hypocrisy: 'Harry tells us that four years of counselling has made him all better! Harry is therapized, Americanised and ready to go, becoming one of our specialties: a self-help guru who's really only in it to sate his narcissism.' Callahan also claimed Harry was blissfully unaware that his 'psychobabble' was diminishing his value on the open market.

SAM WOLFSON was much more compassionate in *The Guardian* (January 2023), arguing that therapy has been weaponised against Prince Harry (pictured above at a Heads Together event). 'If we are serious about removing the stigma around mental health, it cannot be enough simply to start a conversation; we must also reckon with where that conversation goes,' Wolfson wrote.

'In Harry's case, it has led to realisations about a cruel and sometimes abusive childhood... he was refused a hug or even eye contact from his father as he was told about his mother's death, forced to parade publicly behind his mother's coffin, told by his father he was a back-up, and that he might not even be his real son... Is [Harry] a bit weird, with a tendency towards defensive poshness? Absolutely. Is it any wonder why? Not at all.'

ONE OF the most memorable stories in *Spare* concerns Harry's 'todger' which was frozen on a trek to the North Pole. Upon his return, shortly before Prince William's wedding, one of Harry's mates suggested Elizabeth Arden cream which, coincidentally, has a royal warrant. The smell of the cream reminded Harry of his mother, who used it on her lips. 'I felt as if my mother was right there in the room,' Harry wrote. 'Then I took a smidge and applied it…down there.' The Freudian implications are inescapable.

(Apropos male appendages, fans of J K Rowling's most famous character, described as 'Hamlet of the 21st century', should Google 'Changing wand to penis in Harry Potter'.)

Antigone imploring Oedipus not to curse her brothers

For readers unfamiliar with Freud's discredited (but still fascinating) Oedipus complex, and the Greek tragedy which inspired it, suffice to say that the accursed Prince of Corinth unknowingly kills his father, marries his mother, goes mad, blinds himself, and then curses his two sons (who kill each other). As for the mother-obsessed Prince Harry, he once targeted his father's car with a fighter jet during a training mission near Sandringham; and, by his own admission, Harry has struggled with his mental health. Life imitating art? Or confirmation of his curse?

Henry IV's illegitimate granddaughter Antigone, named after Oedipus' daughter, is Prince Harry's ancestor through Henry Spencer (See Page 62).

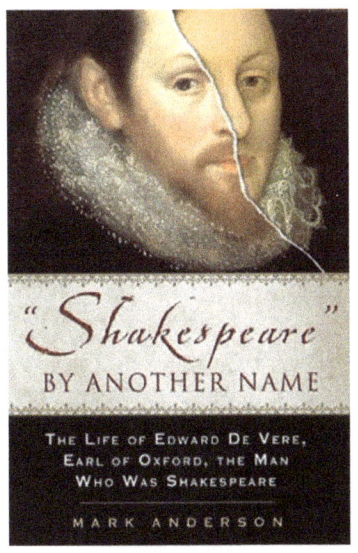

SIGMUND FREUD firmly believed that Prince Harry's ancestor Edward de Vere, the 17th Earl of Oxford - who had a lot in common with the fictional Hamlet - wrote all of the plays attributed to Shakespeare. The so-called Oxfordian theory inspired the 2011 film *Anonymous* and is now widely accepted by non-experts.

Much less believable is the notion that Oxford was an illegitimate son of Thomas Seymour and the future Elizabeth I (who may have been Henry VIII's daughter and granddaughter through Anne Boleyn's mother Elizabeth). And, believe it or not, there is yet another theory that Oxford sired the Virgin Queen's bastard son Henry Wriothesley. That is a lot of incest!

Henry Wriothesley and Henry Carey

PRINCE HARRY descends from Henry Wriothesley, reputedly the 'Fair Youth' in Shakespeare's sonnets, and also from Henry VIII's and Mary Boleyn's alleged bastard son Henry Carey, whose mistress Amelia Bassano — mother of Carey's bastard son Henry Lanier — may have been Shakespeare's mysterious 'Dark Lady'.

In 2024, Daniel Fridell proposed a film depicting the Dark Lady as an actual black woman, possibly Lucy Negro who inspired the 'half-breed' prostitute in the 2005 TV drama *A Waste of Shame*. In other words, it is remotely possible that a woman resembling Meghan Markle inspired one of Harry's ancestors to write the world's most famous love sonnets (See next page).

Regarding Amelia Bassano, John Hudson postulated in 2014 that she 'was in all the right places and had all the right knowledge, skills and contacts to have produced the Shakespearean canon'. Adding to the intrigue, Amelia had an affair with Shakespeare contender Christopher Marlowe whose *Doctor Faustus* is often compared to *Hamlet* and *Oedipus Rex* (acclaimed by Arthur Miller as the two greatest plays ever written).

Harry has read none of these plays but, thanks to Freud, he will forever be linked to them.

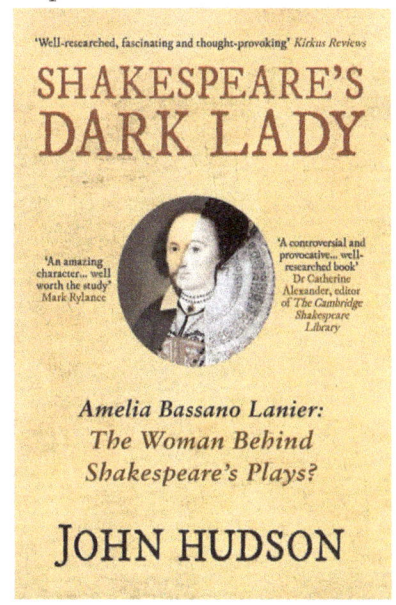

William Shakespeare

> In the old age, black was not counted fair,
> Or, if it were, it bore not beauty's name;
> But now is black beauty's successive heir,
> And beauty slandered with a bastard shame.
>
> For since each hand hath put on nature's power,
> Fairing the foul with art's false borrowed face,
> Sweet beauty hath no name, no holy bower,
> But is profaned, if not lives in disgrace.
>
> Therefore my mistress' eyes are raven black,
> Her eyes so suited, and they mourners seem
> At such who, not born fair, no beauty lack,
> Sland'ring creation with a false esteem.
>
> Yet so they mourn, becoming of their woe,
> That every tongue says beauty should look so.

Elizabeth Vernon

THE NOTION that Prince Harry descends from William Shakespeare of Stratford-Upon-Avon, however far-fetched, is simply too good to ignore.

According to a German professor named Hildegard Hammerschmidt-Hummel, Shakespeare's Dark Lady sonnets were inspired by his lover Elizabeth Vernon who was pregnant with his daughter Penelope when she married the aforementioned 'Fair Youth', Henry Wriothesley, in 1598. Several years earlier, Wriothesley paid a fortune to avoid marrying another Dark Lady contender, also named Elizabeth, who was the oldest daughter of Shakespeare contender Edward de Vere. (It has also been argued that Elizabeth I was the Dark Lady but there is absolutely no proof that she had any children.)

Henry Spencer

Prince Harry descends from Penelope Wriothesley's son Henry Spencer, and also from Henry Rich, son of Penelope Devereux whose other children may have included a bastard son of Henry Wriothesley (possibly the 'bastard shame' in the sonnet above).

Penelope Devereux and Elizabeth de Vere both wore black makeup — 'art's false borrowed face' — while performing in *The Masque of Blackness* before James I. Central to the masque and Shakespeare's sonnets — as well as the Song of Solomon, quoted from at Harry and Meghan's wedding (See Chapter 16) — are repugnant, anti-black sentiments which contributed to Megxit in 2020

> GOOD FREND FOR IESVS SAKE FORBEARE,
> TO DIGG THE DVST ENCLOASED HEARE:
> BLESE BE Yᴱ MAN Yᵀ SPARES THES STONES,
> AND CVRST BE HE Yᵀ MOVES MY BONES.

Anyone seeking DNA evidence that Harry descends from William Shakespeare should bear in mind the curse on his grave from which, according to radar scans, someone has already stolen his skull (perhaps to use in a performance of Hamlet). Alas, poor William!

14

Prince Harry's Curse

From Byron to Batman

IT WAS probably inevitable that Prince Harry would one day be compared to Lord Byron, widely regarded as the first modern celebrity, and also to cinematic versions of Batman — a brooding Byronic hero who, coincidentally, had a childhood sweetheart named Rachel (Meghan's real first name).

Referring to 3rd March 1812, when the first parts of *Childe Harold's Pilgrimage* were published in London, Byron said: 'I awoke one morning and found myself famous.' Almost exactly 200 years later, Harry awoke to front-page pictures of him naked in Las Vegas. Also in 2012, Harry attended the premiere of the last film in the allegedly cursed *Dark Knight* trilogy.

As Daniela Elser wrote on news.com.au in April 2024, Childe Harold is 'a wealthy aristocratic bloke who is deeply unhappy and a bit lost so he ditches the UK to try his luck overseas. Remind you of anyone?' Like Byron, Harry has struggled with his mental health, been outspoken on liberal issues, and fought in a foreign war. Byron also had a lot of Hamlet connections (detailed in a 1962 article, available online, by George Wilson Knight).

According to Byron biographer Fiona MacCarthy, the poet was cursed and so was she. In 2003 Fiona wrote in *The Guardian:* 'He certainly believed in it, pointing to the early deaths of his friends, his dogs and his daughter with a doom-laden conviction that he contaminated anything and everyone with which he had close contact. Battered and scarred for life by eight years' work on his biography, I can say the curse of Byron is still alive and well.'

Prince Harry descends from Vlad the Impaler who inspired Bram Stoker's *Dracula* (1897). Stoker was also inspired by John Polidori's *The Vampyre* (1819) which was wrongly attributed (left), mainly because Lord Ruthven was obviously inspired by Lord Byron. (Coincidentally, Harry descends from a real Lord Ruthven who was executed in 1584 after abducting another of Harry's ancestors, the future James I of England.)

Byron, who was also involved in Mary Shelley's creation of *Frankenstein,* wrote a dramatic poem titled *Manfred* (1817) which inspired Darth Vader in

Star Wars. Manfred attracted Sigmund Freud's close attention because it involved sex and narcissism and was based on the Doctor Faustus legend.

HARRY'S 'Faustian bargain' with the media and the public is neatly explained by Darran Anderson in an article at unherd.com: 'In the traditional Faustian transaction, the would-be genius or celebrity sells their soul, knowing that the cost is damnation and believing that the gains will be worth it. With the royals, fame is hereditary, which is as much of a curse as a blessing. The transaction is one-sided. No deal is made and yet the individual assumes precisely the same debt.' The best-known victim of such a deal is Harry's mother.

royalty with the cleverness and panache of Hollywood,' wrote Daniel D'Addario in *Time* magazine in 2017. 'She remains, two decades after her death, perhaps the most compelling practitioner of celebrity in modern history. Her playbook consisted of breaching the walls of celebrity with a frank, intimate air and then retreating back to a studied sort of privacy.'

In the end, as Roxanne Roberts wrote in *The Washington Post*, Diana was the victim of 'an insatiable celebrity culture and her own tragic misunderstanding of what it meant to be a fairytale princess in the real world.' Harry has been haunted by Diana's death in a Paris road tunnel since 1997 and his biggest fear is that 'history will repeat itself' (hence Harry's overreaction to an allegedly 'catastrophic' car chase by paparazzi in New York in May 2023.)

THE FIRST royal to achieve celebrity status was Edward VIII whose bizarre relationship with Wallis Simpson holds many lessons for Prince Harry (See Chapter 16). Harry can also learn from Edward's war with the media, as outlined by Adrian Phillips in his 2023 book. 'Edward VIII was a child of the burgeoning age of media and the first celebrity monarch,' Phillips wrote, 'but the immense personal popularity created by his charm and good looks was not enough to save him when he came into conflict with a government that embodied the conservative ethos of the time. Nor did the support of powerful media barons.'

William Randolph Hearst, who inspired *Citizen Kane*, dreamed of giving Britain an American Queen. Meanwhile, in Britain, the Anglo-Canadian magnate Lord Beaverbrook hoped the abdication crisis would force his bitter enemy, Prime Minister Stanley Baldwin, out of power. There was no support from George VI and Queen Elizabeth who made sure that Wallis Simpson never became Her Royal Highness. The Duke of Windsor spent the rest of his life trying to air his grievances but died in exile in 1972, having achieved absolutely nothing (and with Wallis refusing to attend his bedside). As a former soldier, Harry should know that some battles are not worth fighting.

Harry and Meghan are fully responsible for their current predicament because they could have chosen to remain out of the spotlight. Instead, they launched an all-out assault on the royal family — in the Oprah interview, in Harry's memoir *Spare,* and also on Netflix. The Sussexes have been courting publicity ever since, while at the same time bemoaning intrusions on their privacy (hence the mockery on *South Park*).

'At the brink of escape, Harry decided to return to the table to sign the contract,' Darran Anderson wrote. Like all Faustian bargains, it will have a bad ending (probably justified after Harry accused other royals of 'getting into bed with the devil'). It is also ironic that one of the Sussexes' biggest problems with their media empire has been an alleged curse: 'so much content, but we only care about the Windsors' (Marina Hyde, *The Guardian,* June 2023).

WHILE preparing for *The Batman* (2022), Robert Pattinson (above) — best known for playing vampire Edward Cullen in the *Twilight* film series — was inspired by Prince Harry. In particular, Pattinson was told that, rather than a playboy, Bruce Wayne — who retreats from civic duties after losing his parents at a young age — should be portrayed as a 'wealthy screw-up.'

Harry's obsession with the caped crusader was obvious at a party held by *Friends* star Courteney Cox where he met actor Will Arnett who featured in the *The Lego Batman Movie* (2017). After several tequilas, Harry kept pestering Arnett to say 'Hello, Harry' in his 'perfect gravelly Batmanese'. 'He wanted to say no, but he didn't want to be impolite,' Harry wrote in *Spare*. 'Or else he recognised that I wouldn't stop.'

Harry's favourite *Friends* actor was Matthew Perry who sold his soul to get the part of Chandler Bing: 'Please, God, make me famous. You can do anything you want to me; just make me famous. Three weeks later, I got *Friends,* and God did not forget about the second part.' After a long battle with alcoholism and drug abuse, Perry committed suicide in October 2023.

The *Friends* episode titled 'The One Where Chandler Can't Cry' involved a pornographic video featuring 'Buffay the Vampire Layer'. Note also that, some years later, when Harry and Prince William pestered Matt LeBlanc about a *Friends* reunion, the actor reportedly told the brothers to 'f… off'. Lord Byron would have said something similar, but more poetically.

15 'The Past is Never Dead'

Prince Harry's Curse

WILLIAM FAULKNER'S famous words about the past sit alone opposite the first page of Harry's memoir. When Harry discovered this quotation on brainyquote.com he was 'thunderstruck' and thought: 'Who the fook (sic) is Faulkner?'

Also relatable to Harry are three other famous quotes: Mark Twain's 'History never repeats itself but it rhymes'; Oscar Wilde's 'Life imitates art far more than art imitates life'; plus Ernest Hemingway's advice to authors: 'Write hard and clear about what hurts'.

(Note that the doomed protagonist in Hemingway's *The Snows of Kilimanjaro* is named Harry; that the insane gold miner in Twain's short story *A Californian Tale*, and the incestuous murderer in Faulkner's biblically inspired *Absalom, Absalom!*, are both named Henry; and that in Wilde's *The Picture of Dorian Gray* the 'devil' is named Lord Henry.)

A good starting point is the 2011 film *Midnight in Paris* (coincidentally the time and place of Princess Diana's fatal accident) because the director, Woody Allen — who once said that 'history is the same thing over and over again' — was unsuccessfully sued by William Faulkner's estate because of a slight misquotation ('The past is NOT dead etc...).

Proving that everything related to Harry is connected, *Midnight in Paris* featured Corey Stoll as Hemingway who, like Faulkner, was greatly influenced by both Mark Twain and Joseph Conrad (more on him shortly). And Allen, who controversially married his stepdaughter, reportedly wanted to work with Princess Diana because she had a 'classy face'.

IN 2021, Prince Harry complained to *People* magazine about the media's mistreatment of Meghan. 'My mother was chased to her death while she was in a relationship with someone that wasn't white and now look what's happened. You want to talk about history repeating itself; they're not going to stop until [Meghan] dies.'

As for life imitating art, here is a quote from *The Hill's* 2024 article about Harry and Meghan's 'royal' visit to Nigeria 'Unfortunately, Harry and Meghan remain self-servingly lost in propagating a dystopian *Heart of Darkness* that in reality ostensibly no longer exists. Western imperialism and racism of old are not destroying modern-day Africa. Rather, Russian and Chinese military and economic imperialism are subjugating sub-Saharan Africa, increasingly through violence and anti-democratic oppression.' While the claim about modern-day imperialism is true, invoking *Heart of Darkness* against Harry and Meghan in this way is unwarranted and unfair.

FOR ANYONE unacquainted with Joseph Conrad's classic novel, which inspired the film *Apocalypse Now, Heart of Darkness* features a fictional ivory trader named Kurtz who goes insane and terrorises part of the Congo region owned by a real-life king, the despicable Leopold II of Belgium.

It has long been debated whether Conrad's book is racist, as famously claimed by Nigerian writer Chinua Achebe in 1975. Interestingly, Barack Obama agreed with Achebe but read *Heart of Darkness* 'to help me understand just what it is that makes white people so afraid. Their demons. The way ideas get twisted around. It helps me understand how people learn to hate.' Harry interviewed Obama on BBC radio in 2017.

Prince Albert and Leopold II

As revealed in the 2016 *Victoria* TV series, her consort Prince Albert may have been sired by Leopold II's namesake father, and not by the older Leopold's brother Ernest I, Duke of Saxe-Coburg and Gotha. If so, Harry's great-great-great-great-grandfather was a half-brother of the evil monarch who killed up to ten million people while looting ivory and rubber from what is now the Democratic Republic of Congo.

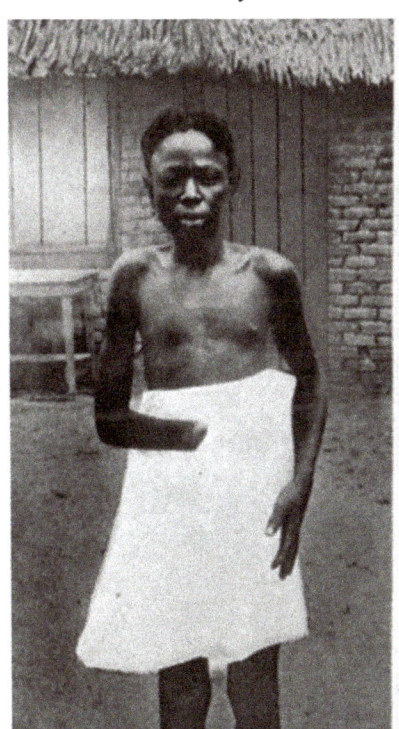 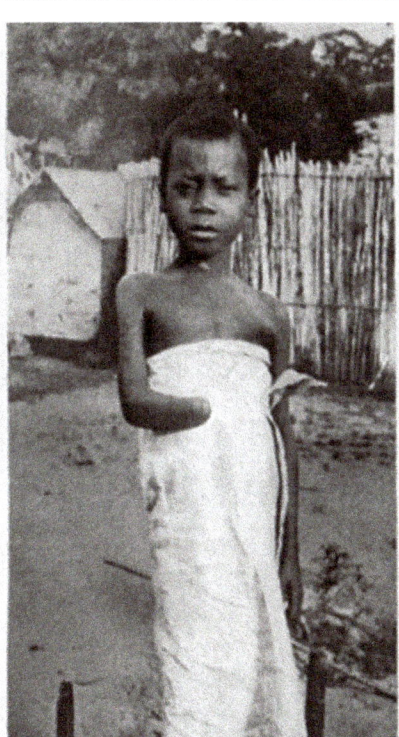 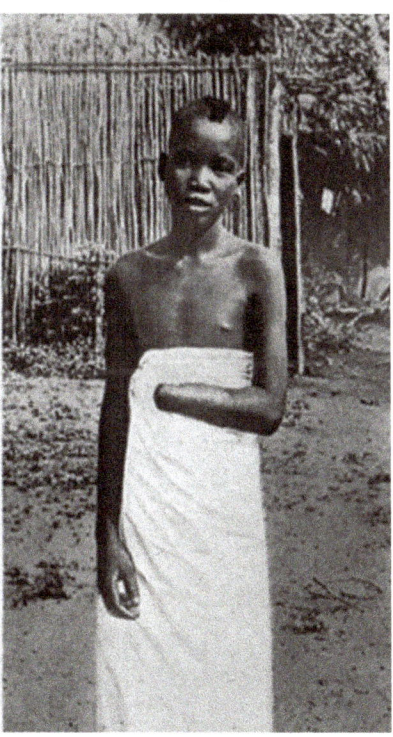

HORRIFIC photographs of mutilated children, punished for not working hard enough on King Leopold's plantations, were published by Mark Twain who wrote: 'In fourteen years Leopold has deliberately destroyed more lives than have suffered death on all the battlefields of this planet for the past thousand years.' Twain called the Belgian king a 'bloody monster whose mate is not findable in human history anywhere'.

In some respects, Britain's colonial record is not much better than Belgium's. Consider, for example, what happened in Kenya while Prince Harry's father was growing up. In January 2023, Mehdi Alavi detailed British atrocities, including ethnic cleansing plus 'forced labor, beatings, starvation, and sexual abuse.' One of those tortured was Obama's grandfather. (Source: fairobserver.com)

IN HIS memoir, Prince Harry describes a fight during which brother William allegedly said that Africa was 'his thing' and that he should have all the elephants and rhinos.

'There are dark historical echoes here,' wrote Nels Abbey in *The Guardian*, 'going all the way back to Europe's imperialist "scramble for Africa". Oneupmanship among European royalty and empires was always a driving objective. In a reflection of how far things have changed yet remained the same, the exchange between the princes appeared to reveal a more intense interest in African wildlife than the African people.'

A feature of Prince Harry's curse is that good intentions often have terrible consequences. The scandal involving atrocities in the Odzala-Kokoua national park in the Republic of Congo is a good example. Condemnation of Harry (currently a director of African Parks) for remaining silent about these allegations is unfair, firstly because he had no personal involvement, and secondly because his commitment to saving African wildlife is well documented.

In 2015, Harry posted about the horrors of rhino poaching in South Africa's Kruger national park: 'Some poachers use a dart gun and tranquilise the animal so as to not have to fire a shot that would be heard. They then hack their face off while the animal is paralysed before running off with the horn.'

THIS QUOTE is reminiscent of a passage in *Heart of Darkness:* 'The word "ivory" rang in the air, was whispered, was sighed. You would think they were praying to it. A taint of imbecile rapacity blew through it all, like a whiff from some corpse. By Jove! I've never seen anything so unreal in my life. And outside, the silent wilderness surrounding this cleared speck on the earth struck me as something great and invincible, like evil or truth, waiting patiently for the passing away of this fantastic invasion.'

Harry helped to relocate elephants in Malawi in 2016

THE OFFENSIVENESS of the title should not stop discussion of Conrad's novel, especially when Mark Twain used the N-word repeatedly in *The Adventures of Huckleberry Finn*, apparently to expose racism, and when Meghan Markle — who has been unfairly accused of narcissism (See next chapter) — vividly remembers an incident in a car park.

'I was home in LA on a college break,' Meghan recalled, 'when my mom was called the N-word. We were leaving a concert and she wasn't pulling out of a parking space quickly enough for another driver. My skin rushed with heat as I looked to my mom. Her eyes welling with hateful tears, I could only breathe out a whisper of words, so hushed they were barely audible: "It's OK, Mommy".'

Prince Charles' toothpaste-squeezing valet (and possible lover), Michael Fawcett, was accused of racism in 2001 after he allegedly called Elizabeth Burgess a 'fucking nigger typist'. 'I never felt part of the team,' she said. 'There were always black jokes and names going round. Because it is the royal family, it is still very protected. It has its own rules and regulations.'

Princess Diana reportedly hated Fawcett and Prince Harry has described his influence as 'pernicious'.

Note: A Latin poem titled Narcissus, about a young man who perishes through self-love, was dedicated to Harry's ancestor Henry Wriothesley (possibly Shakespeare's 'Fair Youth' whose wife Elizabeth Vernon was possibly the 'Dark Lady'). Henry and Elizabeth may also have inspired *Romeo and Juliet).*

16

Something About Meghan?

MEGHAN MARKLE has been well and truly cursed since 2016 when 'a wave of abuse and harassment' resulted in a groundbreaking statement from Prince Harry's spokesman. The statement highlighted a 'smear on the front page of a national newspaper; the racial undertones of comment pieces; and the outright sexism and racism of social media trolls and web article comments.'

Harry was worried about Meghan's safety and deeply disappointed that he had not been able to protect her. 'It is not right that a few months into a relationship with him that Ms Markle should be subjected to such a storm,' the statement said. 'He knows commentators will say this is "the price she has to pay" and that "this is all part of the game." He strongly disagrees. This is not a game — it is her life and his.'

Needless to say, Harry's plea achieved nothing and it was not totally surprising when the statement disappeared from the royal website in December 2023.

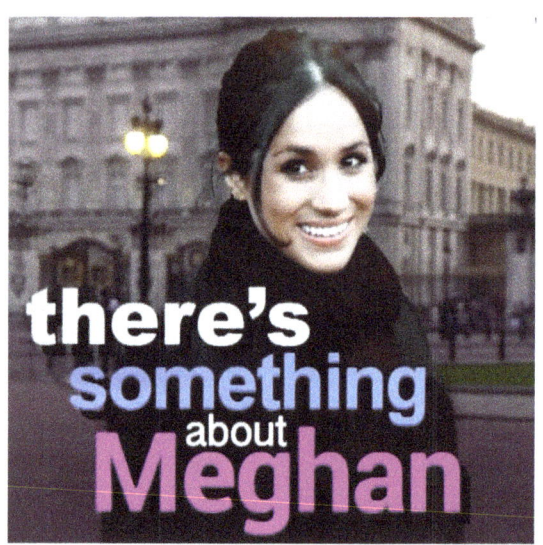

The bizarre (and racist) claim that Harry married Meghan after she and her mother cast a voodoo spell on him was a classic case of history repeating. In 1464, Elizabeth Woodville and her mother Jacquetta of Luxembourg - who claimed descent from the legendary Melusine — allegedly put a spell on Harry's ancestor Edward IV. In 1536, Anne Boleyn was falsely accused of bewitching another of Harry's ancestors, Henry VIII; and exactly 400 years later, American divorcee Wallis Simpson was seen as a wicked witch who cast a spell on Harry's great-great-uncle Edward VIII.

One American commentator invented the 'Yoko Ono curse', accusing Meghan of trying to break up the British monarchy just as Yoko broke up the Beatles. As shown above, Meghan has also been accused of deliberately copying a famous photo of Yoko and John Lennon.

Yoko, now aged 91, once said: 'People accuse artists of being narcissists — of course we are! If we don't like ourselves, who's going to like us?' Meghan has been labelled a narcissist but, while she may tick some of the boxes, she should be given the benefit of the doubt (and the same applies to Harry's unofficial ADHD diagnosis.)

So what are the odds that the Sussexes will stay together like John and Yoko and the Duke and Duchess of Windsor? Based on Harry and Meghan's family histories, very low indeed.

Doria (above) and Thomas Markle separated when Meghan was aged two. The split lacked bitterness, but it did cause emotional damage which Meghan expressed in a poem: ' From Monday to Friday, I'm everywhere… often times it makes me sad… I cannot cry or even scream.'

Despite Meghan's marriage to Trevor Engelson ending in divorce in 2014, she seemingly had a wonderful life, 'passing as white', starring in the *Suits* TV series, and quietly supporting her favourite charities. All that changed when Meghan met Harry (after reportedly setting her sights on Prince William).

DIANA
THE CURSE OF THE SPENCERS

THE MARRIAGE of Prince Charles and Princess Diana was supposedly doomed because of the so-called 'Curse of the Spencers' detailed in a 2022 TV documentary. The eighth Earl Spencer and Frances Roche divorced when Diana was seven years old; her mother divorced second husband Peter Shand Kydd in 1990; her father divorced second wife Raine McCorquodale two years later; and the first three marriages of Diana's brother, Charles Spencer, have also ended in divorce.

Compounding the Spencer curse, Prince Harry's parents were victims of the 'Windsor curse' which struck during 1992, known ever since as Elizabeth II's 'annus horribilis'. A huge fire at Windsor Castle coincided with the marital break-ups of three of the Queen's children: Prince Charles separated from Diana; Prince Andrew separated from Sarah Ferguson; and Princess Anne divorced Mark Phillips.

In a 2020 article in *The Herald* titled "The curse of the House of Windsor', Neil Mackay wrote: 'The Windsors try desperately to love as others do but their position prevents them from doing so. As a result two things happen – they become wounded human beings, and the institution of the monarchy is simultaneously wounded in the eyes of the British people for its cruelty and coldness… The curse seems to hand itself down from generation to generation.'

UNFORTUNATELY for Meghan, it seems that everything involving her is immediately smothered in controversy. In 2019, on mamamia.com.au, Polly Taylor explained how Meghan had been found 'single-handedly responsible for drought, murder and environmental devastation thanks to her breakfast of choice, avocado on toast'.

'[Meghan's] entire pregnancy was scrutinised,' Polly wrote. 'She was unable to place her hands on her blooming baby bump without being accused of milking every photo op. Even her choice to give birth on her own terms, to opt out of the traditional photoshoot mere hours after giving birth, was heavily criticised. And since baby Archie was born, she's been accused of everything from holding him incorrectly, to abandoning him to watch a tennis match. Meghan Markle's life is now the media circus Diana's once was.'

Solomon and a black Sheba

WAS quoting from the Song of Solomon at Harry and Meghan's wedding a bad omen? The passage read by American bishop Michael Bruce Curry was truly romantic: 'Set me as a seal upon your heart, as a seal upon your arm; for love is as strong as death, passion fierce as the grave.'

But what about these controversial words from an earlier passage: 'I am black, but comely, O ye daughters of Jerusalem'. The word BUT — chosen by translators appointed by Harry's ancestor James I, when there were other alternatives — seemingly implies that a woman can not be black AND beautiful. That is the essence of racism.

It has long been debated whether the legendary Queen of Sheba, one of more than a thousand women that Solomon (Harry's alleged ancestor) reputedly slept with, was white or black. Interestingly, the Yoruba people of Nigeria — all possibly related to Meghan — claim that they descend from Sheba, whose alleged burial place is in the village of Oke-Eri in Ogun State. (Note that a curse reportedly prevents any women from seeing the grave.)

Harry and Meghan's 2024 Nigerian visit — to promote the Invictus Games and to improve mental health — is still embroiled in controversy, not least because Elizabeth II was adamant that Harry and Meghan could not be 'half-in and half-out' of the royal family. As well, Meghan copped a lot of criticism for wearing an inappropriate backless 'Windsor gown' (deeply ironic because the Nigerian visit was compared to the Duke and Duchess of Windsor's meeting with Hitler in Germany in 1937).

Like his great-great-uncle, Harry has chosen to live in exile with an American divorcee who seemingly has a psychological hold over her husband. The pressure on their marriage is enormous and there are signs that not all is well at Montecito.

17 Harry's Accursed Namesakes

Prince Harry's Curse

PRINCE HARRY has dozens of royal namesakes — including his ancestors Henry I, II, III, IV, VII and VIII — who were all cursed in one way or another. Many namesakes died young, or else their firstborn sons died young, and most of the others had unnatural deaths. Legitimate or otherwise, they were all tainted with bloodlines from William the Bastard who seized the throne from King Harold (which is Prince William's nickname for Harry).

The future Charles III must have known a lot of this history when he was contemplating names for his second son, already afflicted with 'the curse of the royal spare'. After Charles' first choice, Albert, was vetoed by Princess Diana, they settled on Henry (knowing full well that he would be called Harry).

For more than a thousand years, and around the world, countless commoners named Henry (or variations thereof) have led curse-free lives, but the following list suggests that Prince Harry, like nearly all of Britain's royal Henrys, is doomed.

HENRY I (left): Seemingly cursed after succeeding (and possibly murdering) his older brother William Rufus, Henry lost his only legitimate son, 17-year-old William Adelin, when the White Ship sank in 1120. Henry should have been succeeded by his only legitimate daughter, Matilda, but the throne was seized by her cousin Stephen, resulting in two decades of bloodshed known as The Anarchy.

HENRY FITZROY, one of around ten bastard sons of Henry I, died in 1158 while fighting in Wales on behalf of his nephew Henry II. Prince Harry has a maternal bloodline from Fitzroy through another Henry Fitzroy who was a bastard son of Charles II. Henry, son of Henry I's illegitimate daughter Alice Fitzroy, died young before 1160.

HENRY II was afflicted with the so-called 'Angevin curse' that resulted in rebellious sons, including Richard the Lionheart and King John. Henry's firstborn son, William, died in infancy in 1156. And just over 20 years later, Henry's second son, Henry the Young King, had a firstborn son (also named William) who lived for only three days. The younger Henry, who had reddish-gold hair, died in 1183 aged 28,

Henry II and Henry, the Young King

Henry, second son of Henry II's daughter Eleanor, died in infancy before 1184; and Eleanor's youngest son, also named Henry, died aged 13 in 1217.

HENRY III was weak and ineffectual in accordance with the Prophecy of the Six Kings which labelled him a 'lamb'. He was devastated when his youngest daughter and his oldest granddaughter — both named Katherine — died in infancy just a few years apart.

HENRY OF ALMAIN, nephew of Henry III, was murdered in 1271 by two of his Montfort cousins in revenge for the deaths of their father and oldest brother (Henry de Montfort) at the Battle of Evesham in 1265.

Henry, the second son of Henry III's oldest son Edward I, died aged 6 in 1274. And Henry, third Earl of Lancaster — second son of Henry III's second son Edmund Crouchback — went blind aged about 50 in 1330 and died 15 years later.

HENRY 'HOTSPUR' PERCY — a great-great-great-grandson of Henry III, and one of a long line of Henry Percys — was killed aged 39 at the Battle of Shrewsbury in 1403. Contrary to Shakespeare's play, Hotspur was not killed by the future Henry V. One possibility is that, like King Harold at the Battle of Hastings, Hotspur was struck in the face by an arrow. Hotspur's son and grandson, both named Henry, also died in battle.

HENRY IV, the fourth son of Edward III's fourth son John of Gaunt, usurped the throne from Richard II and was cursed accordingly. Firstly, in the Prophecy of the Six Kings, Henry IV was a mole — which could explain his bad skin, possibly caused by leprosy. Secondly, as a great-great-grandson of Philip IV of France, Henry was a possible victim of the famous Templar curse laid by Jacques de Molay as he burned to death in 1314. (The curse, which lasted 13 generations, also encompassed

Henry V, Henry VI, Henry VII and Henry VIII.) Prince Harry descends from Henry IV's illegitimate granddaughter Antigone (named after Oedipus Rex's daughter).

CARDINAL HENRY BEAUFORT, a bastard half-brother of Henry IV, was afflicted with the same curse as his three Beaufort siblings: they were twice legitimated but barred from holding the throne. Prince Harry descends from Sir Harry Stradling, son of the cardinal's illegitimate daughter Joan (or Jane) whose first cousin - Henry Beaufort, the second Earl of Somerset - died aged 16 in 1418 at the Siege of Rouen. Henry Beaufort's nephew, Henry Courtenay, was beheaded for treason in 1469.

HENRY V. Doomed by the Windsor 'prophecy' to have a short life, Henry IV's firstborn son was glorified by Shakespeare but, in reality, he was a war criminal who had a dubious claim to the throne and an even more dubious claim to France.

HENRY VI (right), who was doomed to have a long but inglorious reign, may have inherited his madness from his grandfather, Charles VI of France. Henry was murdered in 1471 soon after his only son, Edward of Westminster, was killed aged 17 at the Battle of Tewkesbury (won by Edward IV who had a short-lived older brother named Henry of York).

HENRY BEAUFORT, who allegedly slept with both Edward IV and Henry VI's wife, was beheaded at the Battle of Hexham. Prince Harry descends from Beaufort's illegitimate son, and from Edward IV's illegitimate daughter.

Henry VIII, Henry VII, Elizabeth of York and Jane Seymour

HENRY VII: Regardless of whether he was afflicted with the 'King's Curse' laid by his wife and his mother-in-law, Henry VII paid a heavy price after usurping the throne from Richard III. Henry lost his firstborn son Arthur aged 15 in 1502, possibly from the sweating sickness (known as the 'Tudor curse').

HENRY VIII's firstborn son Henry, Duke of Cornwall, died aged just 52 days in 1511. More than twenty years later, having failed to produce a male heir — possibly because he was cursed with Kell positive blood — Henry divorced Catherine of Aragon so he could marry Anne Boleyn (sister of Mary Boleyn, mother of Henry VIII's alleged illegitimate son Henry Carey who sired a bastard son named Henry Lanier).

Henry Carey

HENRY FITZROY (left), Henry VIII's only acknowledged bastard son, was made Duke of Richmond and Somerset and could have been Henry IX if he had not died aged 17 in 1536. One theory is that Fitzroy, Henry VIII's older brother Arthur and Henry's only surviving legitimate son Edward VI, all inherited cystic fibrosis which is similar to tuberculosis.

HENRY COURTENAY, a grandson of Edward IV, was executed in 1539 with Henry Pole, the first Baron Montague, for alleged involvement in the Exeter Conspiracy against Henry VIII. Henry Pole was a hypothetical Henry VII (based on Edward IV's illegitimacy); and Pole's namesake son, who died young in 1542, was a hypothetical Henry VIII.

HENRY BRANDON, a nephew of Henry VIII who died aged 10 or 11 in 1534, should not be confused with Brandon's younger brother, also named Henry, who died aged 6 in 1522. Henry VIII's great-nephew, Henry Clifford, died in infancy.

HENRY STUART, LORD DARNLEY, the obnoxious teenaged great-grandson of Henry VII who married Mary Queen of Scots (his half-first cousin) in 1565, was strangled and blown up two years later after trying to make himself king.

Darnley's handsome and popular grandson, Prince Henry Frederick, died from typhoid fever aged 18 in 1612, dooming James I's spare son Charles I who was beheaded in 1649 (twenty years after his firstborn son lived for just a few hours).

HENRY STUART (right), the childless younger brother of Charles II and James II who nearly became Henry IX after the execution of Charles I, died aged 20 from smallpox in 1660.

HENRY FITZROY, a bastard son of Charles II, died from a battle wound in Ireland in 1690 aged 27. Prince Harry descends from Fitzroy's son Charles who had two namesake sons: one who died in infancy and another who was illegitimate.

PRINCE HENRY (above), a childless younger brother of George III, had several mistresses, including an actress named Ann Elliot, before his marriage to commoner Anne Horton prompted the *Royal Marriages Act* 1772 (which necessitated Elizabeth II's permission for Harry to marry Meghan).

HENRY FITZCLARENCE, one of ten illegitimate children of William IV and actress Dorothea Jordan, died unmarried aged 22 in India in 1817 while serving with the British army. According to Wikipedia, William IV's older brother George IV and songwriter Lady Anne Lindsay may also have had an illegitimate son named Henry, tentatively identified as Captain Henry Augustus Frederick Hervey who died in India in 1824.

HEINRICH, son of Prince Henry of Prussia and Princess Irene of Hesse, inherited haemophilia from his great-grandmother, Queen Victoria, and died aged four in 1904. Other victims of the 'royal curse' included two sons of Prince Henry of Battenberg who married Victoria's daughter Princess Beatrice. (Note that Victoria and Prince Albert were first cousins and so were Heinrich's parents.)

HENRY, son of George V and brother of George VI, was the father of 30-year-old Prince William of Gloucester who died childless in a plane crash in 1972, four years after being diagnosed with porphyria (the 'curse of British royalty' which allegedly caused George III's madness).

PRINCE HARRY is much closer to becoming Henry IX than most people realise. As royal expert Robert Jobson pointed out in July 2024, cancer-stricken Charles III does not want Prince William flying in a helicopter with Kate and their three children. 'Charles insisted that [William] sign a formal document, acknowledging the risks involved and taking full responsibility for his actions,' Jobson wrote, adding: 'It would be scant consolation, of course, for an unspeakable tragedy, let alone for the prospect of King Harry and Queen Meghan.'

AFTERWORD

WHILE Harry may have been less cursed with a different first name, he would still be a red-headed royal spare burdened with all the other afflictions outlined in this book.

As mentioned in the foreword, I ultimately decided that Harry is the victim of a multi-layered curse. Either way, it doesn't really matter because the end result is exactly the same. As William Faulkner wrote, we all 'labor in webs spun long before we were born, webs of heredity and environment, of desire and consequence, of history and eternity.' That doesn't mean everything is predestined, but the odds are often stacked against us.

History suggests that Harry and Meghan's marriage — like the marriages of their parents — will end in divorce. Maybe that will result in a more peaceful life for Meghan and the children, and with Harry rejoining the royal family in some capacity after reconciling with his father and brother. Undoubtedly, that is what Princess Diana would have wanted. Alternatively, if Harry and Meghan persist with their fake royal tours, he could end up in a worse situation than his uncle, and fellow royal spare, Prince Andrew.

Personally, as a big fan of Heinrich Heine's notion of historic recurrence, I hope that a geriatric Harry succeeds Prince Andrew as Duke of York and joins William V in 2066 at events marking the thousandth anniversary of William the Bastard's defeat of King Harold at the Battle of Hastings.

Is Prince William also the victim of a multilayered curse? That may be the subject of my next book. In the meantime, my most recent book — *The Catherine Code* (2023), about Kate Middleton and her royal namesakes — is available through amazon.com and other outlets.

www.ingramcontent.com/pod-product-compliance
Lightning Source LLC
Chambersburg PA
CBHW061401070526
44583CB00026B/3234